T0278364

PRAISE FOR
QUEERING CONTEMPLATION

"I love this book! Like a mystical experience, as I read it, I felt moved and stirred in ways that cannot be expressed in words. Cassidy Hall offers a flowing meditation on what it means to queer and be queer. *Queering Contemplation* invites readers to view contemplation and mysticism through a fresh lens, a sweeping queer scrutiny. With amazing lucidity, Hall illuminates queerness in such a way that allows us to see how it undergirds interconnections, interdependence, and oneness. *Queering Contemplation* is a book I will continue to reread for the sheer beauty it exposes about queerness and its transformative qualities."

—**Lerita Coleman Brown**, PhD, author
of *What Makes You Come Alive*

"*Queering Contemplation* is a paradigm shifter. Thank you, Cassidy Hall, for returning us to the wise matrix of Western Christian contemplation by synonymizing Mystery, equity, love, interconnectedness, kindness, social justice activism, and abundant, everyday mysticism. Sharing stories and teachings from the overlooked or silenced margins, Hall makes compassionate space for an evolving community of listening and belonging."

—**Carmen Acevedo Butcher**, PhD, poet, and translator
of Brother Lawrence's *Practice of the Presence*
and of *The Cloud of Unknowing*

"In *Queering Contemplation*, Cassidy Hall offers a deep breath to anyone who worries that contemplative practices aren't made for people like them. Her story, as well as the voices of wisdom she weaves throughout the book, will provide fresh insight for both new and experienced lovers of stillness and sanctuary."

—**Austen Hartke**, author of *Transforming: The Bible and the Lives of Transgender Christians*

"*Queering Contemplation* opens a treasure chest of wisdom and perspective. This book is such an incredible contribution to increasingly diverse and inclusive contemplative resources."

—**Rev. Dr. Barbara A. Holmes**, author of *Joy Unspeakable* and core faculty at the Center for Action and Contemplation

"If you simply find yourself not fitting into categories or often marginalized for being weird and odd, then you are one of those magical people Cassidy Hall is encouraging to walk an unencumbered spiritual path. In *Queering Contemplation*, she destroys the societal boxes we have been stuffed into, including those imposed upon us within our spiritual and religious sanctuaries. Hall calls us to dismantle uniformity and mainstreaming prayer and/or meditation so we can engage the Divine from our hearts and not be dictated by those in power who are confined to archaic and patriarchal beliefs. Most importantly, Hall removes the stigma of queerness and places queerness within an essential and open spiritual path of liberation, insight, and illumination—a path to be discovered within everyone."

—**Zenju Earthlyn Manuel**, author of *Opening to Darkness*, *Sanctuary*, and *The Way of Tenderness*

"Cassidy Hall's *Queering Contemplation* is a beautiful and eloquent book, showcasing her articulate and deeply honest voice and vital message. She breaks new ground in making necessary and insightful connections between contemplation, sacred activism, and queerness. This book expanded my understanding of what it means to be contemplative, and to be queer. It's a book I'll return to again and again, and will enthusiastically recommend to others."

—**Carl McColman**, author of *The New Big Book of Christian Mysticism* and *Eternal Heart*

"In our hectic and busy lives, we need a contemplative spirituality now more than ever. Cassidy Hall helps make a future where *everyone* is invited into contemplation. Whether you identify as LGBTQ+ or not, this book will queer your spiritual life."

—**Mason Mennenga**, podcast host of *A People's Theology*

"Certifiably off-center, I celebrated reading this integrated, quietly persuasive book on contemplative prayer as inherently strange and boundary-breaking. Contemplative prayer is a learned, disciplined experience but possibly almost inherent to those who approach life from strange sides, each of them queer in their own way. Cassidy Hall well makes her case that queer contemplative prayer is not an oxymoron. Round of applause, I'd suggest, and from all quarters."

—**Jonathan Montaldo**, author of *Bridges to Contemplative Living with Thomas Merton*

"Cassidy Hall's marvelous book *Queering Contemplation* is part of an exciting and essential expansion of writing about contemplative practice. Read it to embrace your own queerness—those wild parts of you always moving toward greater liberation—and discover how this freedom connects us even more deeply to all of life. This beautifully written work, with its array of wise voices and perspectives, is a must-read for anyone interested in the contemplative path!"

—**Christine Valters Paintner**, PhD, author
of *The Love of Thousands* and other books,
and online abbess at Abbey of the Arts

"Cassidy Hall has managed to do the impossible here in *Queering Contemplation*: create something incredibly precise and yet universally meaningful. Her words are that rare combination of passion and intellect that stir the spirit and engage the mind. This book is essential reading for anyone looking to discover the wild, expansive nature of full authenticity."

—**John Pavlovitz**, pastor, activist, and author
of *If God Is Love, Don't Be a Jerk*

"This is a book of reclamation, adding to the long line of mystics who subverted religious expectation. Hall tells a truer story, offering us both the intimacy of personal sharing and the rigor of research. *Queering Contemplation* is the response to the very human questions that stir in so many of us—*Where do I belong? Is it safe to belong here?* Hall retrains our imaginations for a spirituality that is more strange, more beautiful, and more honest than the doctrines we've often been cornered into."

—**Cole Arthur Riley**, *New York Times*–bestselling author of
This Here Flesh and *Black Liturgies*

"Cassidy Hall reminds us that there are many roads to contemplation, that queer people have a head start in understanding alternative consciousness, and that things are not the way everybody thinks. *Queering Contemplation* is going to help a lot of people."

—**Richard Rohr**, OFM, author of *The Universal Christ*
and other books, and founder of the Center for
Action and Contemplation

"*Queering Contemplation* is a brave endeavor. As a Black, African-descended, cisgendered woman, I am not 'queer' in my sexuality, but I am queer, at least to some, in how I enter the world: as a contemplative and Spirit-led woman, reclaiming my indigenous roots, embracing my community, and using my inherent gifts to serve those who are sent, in noise and in silence, to explore the mystical given to us at birth. How important Cassidy Hall's work is for all of us!"

—**Therese Taylor-Stinson**, author of
Walking the Way of Harriet Tubman

QUEERING CONTEMPLATION

CASSIDY HALL

QUEERING
CONTEMPLATION

Finding Queerness in
the Roots and Future of
Contemplative Spirituality

Broadleaf Books
Minneapolis

QUEERING CONTEMPLATION
Finding Queerness in the Roots and Future of Contemplative Spirituality

Copyright © 2024 Cassidy Hall. Published by Broadleaf Books, an imprint of 1517 Media. All rights reserved. Except for brief quotations in critical articles or reviews, no part of this book may be reproduced in any manner without prior written permission from the publisher. Email copyright@1517. media or write to Permissions, Broadleaf Books, PO Box 1209, Minneapolis, MN 55440-1209.

Library of Congress Cataloging-in-Publication Data

Names: Hall, Cassidy, author.
Title: Queering contemplation : finding queerness in the roots and future of contemplative spirituality / Cassidy Hall.
Description: Minneapolis, MN : Broadleaf Books, [2024] | Includes bibliographical references.
Identifiers: LCCN 2023037167 (print) | LCCN 2023037168 (ebook) | ISBN 9781506493398 (hardcover) | ISBN 9781506493404 (ebook)
Subjects: LCSH: Contemplation. | Queer theology.
Classification: LCC BV5091.C7 H365 2024 (print) | LCC BV5091.C7 (ebook) | DDC 248.3/40866--dc23/eng/20231206
LC record available at https://lccn.loc.gov/2023037167
LC ebook record available at https://lccn.loc.gov/2023037168

Cover design: Hannah Gaskamp
Cover image: gettyimages-1138590668-170667a

Print ISBN: 978-1-5064-9339-8
eBook ISBN: 978-1-5064-9340-4

Dedicated to the queerness
in each of us

CONTENTS

AUTHOR'S NOTE

This book is about my own queer and contemplative journey—
one person's journey. I can only speak for and from my own
experience of queerness and contemplative life. My story is
not a universal experience of queerness, what it means or feels
like to be queer; nor is it a universal experience of contemplative life. I name my social location as a cisgender queer white
woman, because that points toward the experiences I have and
haven't had that make up my worldview. I speak from a position
of privilege, even by the nature of writing a book. While I am
actively unlearning whiteness, ableism, cisnormativity, and other
dominant ways of perceiving the world, that is a lifelong journey.
Along the way, I am learning from those who share their experiences as transgender, two-spirit, intersex, gender-nonconforming,
agender, disabled, immigrants, people of color, and others. In
order to learn from these voices and to share this wisdom, I have
included some of their words and experiences throughout the
book. It is my hope that their voices will give insights into experiences and encounters unlike my own.

In this book I use the term *people of color* to refer to Black,
Indigenous, Asian, Latine, multiracial, and other communities. I don't do this to collapse their experiences into a singular
encounter, but to address the ways my own experience is limited

by my whiteness. My work is ongoing here, and I look forward to the conversations of correction and being called into the truth of the vastness of these experiences.

When "activism" and "activists" are discussed in the book, I am referencing activism focused on the liberation of all people. Most often, I am referring to social-justice activism and activists, from whom I have learned much about my own contemplative life.

This book contains some stories related to anxiety, depression, mental health, and the violence inflicted upon marginalized communities. If those parts might be harmful for you to read, please skip over them as they arise. Unfortunately, by the nature of addressing queerness and contemplation in the world we live in, these realities are a part of the conversation.

You might notice I rarely, if ever, use the word *God* unless I am quoting someone else. This was a choice based on my own experiences of the misuse of *God* and the many ways the word can be distracting. I choose to use the word *Divine* in its place, as an invitation to see the vastness of the Spirit within and around us—not just as something "out there" but something "right here."

After you have read this book, in part or in full, I hope we might all engage our own contemplative lives and the word *queer* differently. Above all, I invite you into your own unfolding, your own exploring, and your own blossoming, in your own way.

1 | LETTING GO OF THE STATUS QUO
Queering Contemplation

> So that contemplation can be whole, it must consist of both inward solitude and reflection, and outward response to the situations in which we find ourselves present and awake.
>
> —Therese Taylor-Stinson, *Ain't Gonna Let Nobody Turn Me Around*

My therapist tells me I'm a plant.

Plants have a way of quietly detoxifying the air in a home, taking in the toxins while putting out fresh air to breathe. We discuss this when we talk about my childhood and the roles I've played in my family. It's not that I didn't contribute to the toxins in my home or that I only put out clean air. But like most empaths and highly sensitive people, I learned to cope with the intensity of exposed or hidden emotions around me, similar to the way a plant can exist amid the noise while emitting its silent attempts at detoxifying the air.

The coping skills, however complicated, that I developed in my family of origin played a part in my moving toward contemplation. True contemplative life, of course, is a way of life and not a coping skill. But my therapist reminds me to find gratitude for the old stories and to seek the gifts from them—and learning contemplation happens to be among the gifts. At the time I didn't know what I was doing in any kind of a formal sense, but I knew it was a place of sacred pause, calm, and clarity.

Reaching back into some of those first memories of contemplation, I see my six-, eight-, ten-year-old self in the rooms of my childhood home. I remember the ways it felt to go into my room to pause, feel big emotions, or go away from others to simply center, gather, or clear my mind. Often, when my emotions or those around me were too overwhelming or altogether unspoken, I'd steady myself with silence or go to my room for stillness. I'd go for a walk into the prairie land behind my childhood home or gaze out the window for centering. Contemplative life was forming within me without any traditional understanding of exactly what it was. However psychologically problematic, these moments became the beginning of understanding what mystic Howard Thurman would have called my "inward sanctuary," and the beginning of my lifelong relationship with contemplative life, though I didn't yet have the language for it.

In those moments of stepping away, I always wanted a companion to join me in that inner sanctuary. I wanted someone to soothe, help, guide, or witness my experience. And I spent so much of my life wondering if they'd ever show up.

Eventually, I came to recognize myself in that inner sanctuary as the first companion I'd been waiting for. The waiting I'd been doing for someone else was the restlessness of moving away from my own feelings, voice, truth, and life. And as I began learning about the inner sanctuary's possibility, I started to recognize my own power more clearly. I began to develop and delve into the ongoing work of healthier emotional regulation. I discovered the ways contemplation connected me to humanity through the roots of life, the roots of the plant. The contemplative companion I'd longed for, in order to be myself, was already within me. While I still wanted and needed others for the journey, I first needed myself. And this companion I found within me also revealed that true contemplative life lives in advocating for both my own roots and the roots of those around me. Now, through vulnerability, a teeming curiosity, embodiment, and interconnection, I continue to step into the rooted contemplative life.

I'd also learn that contemplation is less about what happens to me or around me and more about how I choose to participate in it, or how I pause before I engage. I'd learn that contemplative life is an inner stance, a way of navigating my interior world and the relationships around me. Contemplation can show up as the pause when I gaze at the maple tree billowing in the breeze, my arrival at the state house to protest the latest anti-trans bills and rhetoric, the walk in the woods when I find my body metabolizing memories, the note written to the beloved in silence, the strange bug I see with my nephew on a walk by the ocean, the morning's silent coffee with my companion, the weeping prayer I experience when I sense my interconnectedness to all living beings. Contemplation is the centering of myself in order to know and remember who I am and what I am to speak—or show up to. Contemplative life is a continual deep engagement with the roots and truth of life that bind me to all the lives around me.

In her seminal work, *Joy Unspeakable: Contemplative Practices of the Black Church*, Rev. Dr. Barbara A. Homes writes, "Contemplation is not confined to designated and institutional sacred spaces." Instead, she claims, "activism and contemplation are not functional opposites. Rather, contemplation is, at its heart, a reflective activity that is always seeking the spiritual balance between individual piety and communal justice seeking."

Sometimes contemplation is a place I *go*, sometimes a practice I *do*, and sometimes a place I can *be*. But true contemplative life necessitates a balance and compels us to engage in the ebb and flow between our individual experience and communal wellbeing. Psychotherapist and contemplative Dr. Jim Finley talks about the ways the contemplative path comes to fulfillment in oneness. This oneness—both with oneself and with others—is a way of life worth our continual pursuit.

Much like the plant, whose *be*-ing and emitting of oxygen emerge from its stability of rootedness, contemplation is traditionally understood and defined (here by *Merriam-Webster*) as a rooted or focused "concentration on spiritual things" and an "intention," an "awareness," a "regarding steadily." Spiritually speaking, contemplative life is concerned with both attention and emptiness. To contemplate the matters of the Divine or spirituality often necessitates silence, stillness, and solitude. The origins of the word *contemplation* come from the Latin *contemplatio*, and the Greek *theoria*, *theorein*, both referring to a sense of what B. Alan Wallace calls complete "devotion to revealing, clarifying, and making manifest the nature of reality."

It's no wonder the plant sinks into its task of *be*-ing and, in turn, producing oxygen as it senses the reality of toxins around it. Like the plant's focus and its exchange with its environment, contemplation is a place of awareness, clarity, and navigating reality—birthed from a rootedness of focused attention.

As life's roots vary in size, shape, depth, and experience, so too does contemplative life look and express itself differently for everyone. It is not a one-size-fits-all practice or way of being.

Contemplative life is as unique as the roots of the nearly 400,000 plant species and all the different ways those individual plants show up—each a necessary part of nature's connection and survival. Contemplation can be loud as often as it can be quiet. In fact, contemplative expressions live along—and outside of—spectrums of population, noise, and physical location. While I most often find aloneness, silence, and solitude to be a helpful part of my individual practices of contemplation, that isn't the case for everyone. Dr. Holmes speaks of how contemplation can happen amid noise and can be a communal experience involving shouting or silence.

The assumption that contemplative practice requires silence dates back to the philosopher Plotinus (205–270). But by tethering silence to contemplation, has the dominant culture tried to create a norm for all cultures? Holmes explores this, writing that it is almost as though "we have drawn the spiritual veil around contemplative activity, seeking to distance prayerful and reflective practices from the noise of the world."

So, who has defined what contemplation looks like—and doesn't? Whose voices have historically mattered in the conversations about contemplative practice—and whose haven't? And what would happen if we began to look behind the curtain of the dominant narrative to see the great expanse, the infinite expressions of contemplative life?

What would happen if we queered contemplation?

QUEERLY CONTEMPLATING

At first glance, contemplation and queerness may not seem to be related to each other. But through engaging in the contemplative life, I've come to learn that contemplation makes me *more* queer—more curious, wild, weird, fierce, free, embodied, and present. And, in turn, my queerness—in terms of both my sexuality and strangeness—has given my contemplative life more spaciousness, permission, eroticism, and wonder. My queerness and my contemplative life have become a union of joy, pleasure, and infinite possibility.

Queer is the way I tilt my head to look at the world. Queerness, in my life, has been not only about sexuality but also about expanse, curiosity, openness, pleasure, weirdness, love, oddity, and liberation. I deeply believe queerness lives in every human in the ways we find ourselves subverting the status quo, forgoing norms, and engaging one another with open hearts and hands. By definition, queerness relates to *oddness, strangeness, eccentricity,* and *unconventionality.* While queerness can also relate to non-hetero sexuality or to a gender that is not cisgender (because by its nature queerness refuses categories), this book engages the great expanse of the word. In what ways can all the meanings of queerness awaken contemplation and life?

Because this book and my deeper work are about queering contemplation, it's important to consider what it means to queer something. In my understanding of queer theory—as a philosophy and study of lives and expressions disentangled from heteronormativity—I am seeking to disentangle my own experience of contemplation from the grasp of Western Christian expressions formed in heteronormativity, patriarchy, and Eurocentricity/whiteness. In my exploration of contemplation and mysticism, I hope to cultivate a conversation around the topics of strangeness, oddity, liberation, love, delight, and wonder—disentangled from manipulation, power, abuse, and violence. And these pivots take time. It is a continual process to disentangle ourselves from these dominative foundations; it takes time for us to find our own way and own voice in contemplative life.

WRESTLING RESTLESSNESS

I first arrived at the doorstep of formal contemplative life in 2011, when I began reading the writing of largely straight cis white men whose works were considered the canon of texts. Their books were easily accessible and affordable by the nature of their social location, but their worldviews were limited. These authors and practitioners became the way Western Christian contemplative studies took shape, and their work was my introduction to formal contemplative life, practice, and studies. But much like how I waited in my childhood for the companion of contemplation to join me, I knew something was missing. It would take me years to discover just what that was.

In those years, as I began to dig into the Western Christian contemplative canon, it became clear to me that this particular canon didn't reflect the fullness of my experience as a queer woman in the contemplative life, not to mention countless other experiences and expressions it failed to represent. Not only did most of the widely accepted contemplative work overlook other religions and spiritualities that yielded to contemplation long before Christianity did; as I read more, I found it also failed to consider the ways privileged social locations can cloud the view of contemplation's necessary counterpart: action.

Years later, even as I noticed that something was missing, I became involved with these circles of contemplative life, including serving two terms as the secretary of the International

Thomas Merton Society, a group founded on the work and life of the contemplative Trappist monk Thomas Merton. During this time, I was invited to speak at an event in Chicago memorializing the fiftieth anniversary of Thomas Merton's death.

Reviewing the event's program, I noticed I was one of only two women among an otherwise all-male, all-white list of speakers, and the sole openly queer person invited to speak. Though I wasn't surprised, I began to pay attention to, and witness, the gap: how overlooked people of color, women, and LGBTQIA+ people are by the Western Christian contemplative canon.

Throughout the panel discussion, we were asked about our own feelings about Merton's work, how we felt his work could continue to enliven young people, and if there were any challenges we experienced with things he'd written about. Though I'd only been a part of the Merton world and contemplative circles for a short time, earlier that year at a Toronto bookshop I had come across a book of Merton's letters, which became, again, an unsurprising challenge.

I shared with the group how I had found "homosexuality" written in the index of that book and had become curious. *Homosexuality*, I thought, *but Merton never really wrote about that.* Sure enough, I met with familiar and painfully disappointing words like those that continue to deeply wound and haunt LGBTQIA+ folks daily. In a note titled "Letter to an Unknown Friend," Merton wrote:

> In other words, the pitch is this. Homosexuality is not a more "unforgivable" sin than any other and the rules are the same. You do the best you can, you honestly try to fight

it, be sorry, try to avoid occasions, all the usual things. . . .
Maybe psychiatric help would be of use.

Sharing this story with the group, I felt my body tense up with
the agony, pain, and harm these kinds of words cause. It was the
old feeling of despair tethered to the lies I'd been told by church
leaders of my past: that there was something innately wrong with
me or something sinful about my personhood.

I used to be among those quick to give Merton leeway, saying
things like, "He was a man of his time," or "He was a product
of the Catholic church," or "He would probably think and write
differently today." But that's an avoidance of the issue at hand.
Simply put, Merton was wrong here. And that doesn't need to be
hard to say.

Why is it so difficult to name the fact that sometimes our
teachers hold problematic and even harmful stances? Not all
roots developed in contemplative life connect with and reach
out for the betterment of *all* life. My hope for my own thoughts
and work is that they will be corrected as I age and after I die.
And that my roots will continue to be redirected and strength-
ened to love and protect those around me. With Merton, I've
found that when I fail to express the problems with his words,
I justify and perpetuate the harm of those words. And when I
fail to name that harm, I exacerbate the violence those words
cause.

Although I'll never know what happened in Merton's evolution of thought regarding the LGBTQIA+ community, the fact
remains that the sentiment expressed in this particular book was
wrong, harmful, and violent. Not only was Merton distancing
himself from the personhood of another, he also caused harm

by suggesting that such a lived experience aligned with sin and required help.

An editor I knew attended this same commemoration event. Earlier we had discussed the possibility of a book project about my travels to all seventeen Trappist monasteries in the US. But before the event and our meeting, the editor emailed me, saying their publishing company "would probably view LGBTQ voices as more liability than asset." In a later email, they continued: "I know it sucks. In a few years it will be different." While this *also* wasn't shocking, I was reminded of the ways my voice and truth have companioned me in contemplative life. My voice deserved an authentic spaciousness to express itself, to sink into the roots of contemplative life's possibility. Mainstream Christian contemplation marginalizes others through its platforming of predominantly cis white male teachers and ways of thinking. This is a disservice to the fullness of the contemplative experience. To truly live in rooted contemplation, to truly emit the oxygen of fresh air, I must learn to fight for my roots and those of others in order for us all to exist, thrive, and be heard.

As I began to see the many ways in which this contemplative world perpetuated oppression, silencing, and marginalization in my life and the lives of others, I committed to stepping more deeply into my true self and into learning from others. My curiosity continued to enlarge: How was the contemplative life—a seemingly inclusive way of being—minimizing or diminishing the fullness of others? Recognizing my own participation in this harm, how could I commit to finding a better way?

The voices of the contemplative status quo are not obsolete or altogether unhelpful, but their work can be largely irrelevant for those whose lives they don't reflect or represent. For people like me who have found—or have yet to find—their own voice and companionship in contemplative life, yielding to the contemplative status quo can cloud that discovery. Those who experience daily oppressions, those whose energy must go to survival, and those who live within marginalized communities may find their contemplative expressions underrepresented or entirely nonexistent in the canon of Western Christian contemplative work. Much of the contemplative work I once leaned into depended on the notion that withdrawing from the world was the best way to love it more deeply. But this idea, created by voices of the contemplative status quo, ignored how showing up to our lives and communities can be an act of contemplation, liberation, or even survival (of story or self). For many, including me, contemplation begins right where we are—and going away from the world disregards our responsibility to make it a better place for all of creation.

The work of contemplative monks like Thomas Merton, a straight cisgender white man, cannot express what it's like for me to be a queer woman in America as rights are being stripped away in laws impacting bodily autonomy, marriage equality, and the rights of my trans and gender-nonconforming siblings. The contemplative scholarship of white men such as Bernard McGinn and Martin Laird cannot fathom the experience of people of color or the ways in which the "contemplative practices of the Black Lives Matter movement are a part of the lineage of black communal and church traditions," which Dr. Holmes speaks to. My work or the work of fellow white contemplative Cynthia Bourgeault cannot encompass an understanding of Harriet Tubman as a contemplative mystic in the way Therese

Taylor-Stinson, founder of the Spiritual Directors of Color Network, does.

While all these lived experiences of contemplation can inform one another, and some common beliefs about contemplative life may be found among them, such shared truths cannot be fully expressed until all voices are at the table where they belong.

BREAKING UP WITH THOMAS MERTON

In 2020, upon completion of my film about Thomas Merton's hermitage years, *Day of a Stranger,* I showed it to an audience in Bowling Green, Kentucky. Each time I showed the film or gave a talk on a Merton panel or at a conference, I was asked some form of the question "How can we be sure younger generations learn about Thomas Merton?" Viewers respond to Merton's words as prescient, especially in the case of the stream-of-consciousness recordings I excerpted from his time as a hermit on the grounds of the Abbey of Gethsemani in Kentucky. A kind of anxiety to preserve his voice for future generations has come up at every screening or Merton event I've attended since 2011.

In the past, I responded with encouragement, mentioning Merton's interfaith dialogue, his modeling of friendship, and the expansiveness of his correspondence as the ways his legacy might endure. But at this particular film screening, coming on the heels of much self-reflection on the question, I responded to the person in the audience with my own question: "What's wrong with Merton disappearing?"

It's been almost sixty years since Merton died in Bangkok, shortly after giving a lecture on Marxism and monastic perspectives. At the end of the lecture, referencing a forthcoming Q&A,

he said, "We are going to have the questions tonight. . . . Now, I will disappear." Though it was only a silly little line at the end of a heavy and controversial talk, what if it was also prophetic?

Merton was indeed controversial in his time, and his words remain relevant and helpful for some. But even his most recent work is now more than half a century old. And while his conversation partners spanned gender (Dorothy Day, for example), sexuality (James Baldwin, though it's said he never replied to Merton), religion (Thich Nhat Hanh, Abraham Joshua Heschel, D. T. Suzuki), racial justice (Martin Luther King Jr.), and environmental justice (Rachel Carson), Merton was a straight European cis man who took monastic vows in a patriarchal church, perpetuating damaging exclusivity alongside his wisdom. In truth, his prescience and ecumenism seem rare only when looking at other white spiritual writers of the time or reading exclusively Catholic work from the 1940s–1960s. Perhaps this context makes his views appear more radical than they really were.

From Womanist scholars I have learned to ask a new set of questions: *Whose voice is missing? Who isn't yet at the table? Who can speak to this from a different set of experiences, from roots unlike my own?* Because as long as I perpetuate the domination of only a few voices in Western Christian contemplative work, I hinder movement toward all voices being heard. I cannot learn from Merton what it feels like to be trans in America being denied health care, or what it means to be an LGBTQIA+ person rejected by a church, or to be Black in America, or to face AAPI racism, or to be a refugee turned around or arrested at the border. The old Western Christian contemplative canon, including Merton, can provide historical perspective and observations, but most often cannot speak into an oppressive situation separate from their identity and experience. It remains unknown where Merton would stand now, but in his lifetime he did seek out new voices, welcomed varying perspectives, and was curious about experiences unlike his own. In that manner, he modeled the necessity of contemplative life to welcome other experiences, views, and voices.

On my way home from that film screening and the anxious question that followed, I decided to take a detour to stop by Gethsemani Abbey. After a rain-soaked hike, I paused at Merton's grave, marked by a simple white cross engraved with "Father Louis," as he was known there. I sensed something of finality to this visit, a kind of saying goodbye. At his grave I recalled other words he wrote in *The Sign of Jonas*: "They can have Thomas Merton," he said of those who assumed they knew all about him solely based on his writing. "He's dead. Father Louis—he's half dead, too."

I believe it's finally time to acknowledge that my long obsession with the words and wisdom of Thomas Merton and other status-quo contemplatives crowded out other voices and perspectives, other roots of depth, preventing me from hearing them fully—starting with my own.

The first companion I'd been waiting for, after all, was myself.

The first voice I'd been needing to hear, it turns out, was mine.

REPOTTING, RENEWING, REBLOOMING

Every time I pull out a plant to repot, I am in awe of what the root system has accomplished. Hidden behind the ceramic, the roots have grounded themselves in the soil, embracing nutrients, communicating with each other, and piercing the terra firma for the plant's own survival. These roots show us the hidden contemplative life of plants. They reveal to us the necessity for stillness, depth, and connection, in order to emit cleaner air for all of us to breathe.

The plant rests in the corner of the room, quietly searching for the sun. I turn to look outside at a tree. Neither the plant nor the tree hurries, and their roots take pause. Indeed, their growth and ability to offer air, flowering, truth, and beauty depend on their sacred pauses, their own inner sanctuary. And that inner sanctuary is not in isolation. Fungi and roots in the soil communicate with all other living things within the surrounding soil and even share nutrients so that all can thrive.

The beauty of plants, trees, and flowers is no coincidence. In fact, their own coming out, much like the coming out of queer folks, is often accompanied by a flowering. I'm always amazed at the way flowers seem to appear overnight, as though they were just plain ready to enter the world on their own terms. So it's not startling that flowers have often symbolized or referenced queer folks. In 1982, the green carnation became such a sign when author Oscar Wilde asked friends to wear them. Another example is the flower imagery in the poems of the queer Greek poet Sappho (c. 630–c. 570)—from whom the word *lesbian* derives, as she lived most of her life on the isle of Lesbos. Then there are the flowering pansies, of course—*pansy* becoming a term for gay men, especially in New York City in the 1920s and 1930s. And lavender is embedded throughout history, from Sappho's implication that it is a color of desire to Rita Mae Brown's reclamation of the term "lavender menace" in 1970, to signify the importance of lesbians in the National Organization for Women.

Not unlike flowers and the roots from which they emerge, contemplation and queerness are both innately blossoming and abundant materials. They root us, ground us, and connect us—allowing our most authentic self to emerge and bud into existence. Contemplation and queerness are democratic in that they are for everyone—invitations into one's truest self. And I believe both queerness and contemplation contain the creative, generative materials necessary to awaken our contemplative life into its innate embodiment, liberative focus, infinite possibility, and autonomous expression.

As a cis queer white woman in a privileged position, I understand that my exploration of contemplation, among all the other topics in this book, is centered more on thriving than on survival, more focused on inclusivity than on liberation. With that realization comes another: even as I discover my own voice, my own companionship, I know I have so much to learn from those whose work centers on survival and liberation—whose contemplative study, lives, and theologies have been birthed from places of deep wisdom unlike my own. Because of this, I hope this book leans into the insights of these voices in order to bring us all closer to contemplative life's potential—in embodiment, practice, and interdependence. I hope that the unified truths about contemplation may be revealed, as voices with varying identities arrive at the table where they belong. Including your voice; including mine.

I'd like to be the plant that digs deep into the gift of contemplation to remember *who I am, what I am to speak—and show up to.* I'd like to be the plant that keeps queerly tilting my head and roots to understand others and myself, to continue expanding and exploring the vast beauty within and around me.

As we all sink into our own unique inner sanctuary, may we keep finding the roots that bind us together. May we share nutrients as we learn to unfold ourselves with the spaciousness of becoming and blooming into who we are.

And wherever your roots, your soil, your body, your leaves, your blossoming, I hope that together, we can reimagine and queer contemplation so that it further provides the nutrients and air for all of us who long for contemplation's expansive invitation.

AN INVITATION TO LET GO OF THE CONTEMPLATIVE STATUS QUO

Alicia Crosby Mack (she/her/hers)

This interview for the *Queering Contemplation* podcast took place on January 30, 2023, on Zoom.

Alicia's work rests at the intersections of the spiritual, systemic, and interpersonal harm people experience. I learned of her passions for justice and engaged activism through her social media accounts and our shared work on the board of enfleshed, an organization focused on spiritual nourishment for collective liberation. When we sat down to talk about all things queer, she shared the ways the premise of queerness existed long before she conceived any definitions of it:

> It's interesting to look back at myself and understand that I've always been queer, even if I didn't have, like, the language or even awareness of language of queerness. For me, queerness means to subvert; it means to be different, to not

be whatever is considered normative in a context. But that subversion theme is important. There are a lot of people who would say things are queer or people are queer, and they're not. I mean, maybe they're a little bit different, but they're not subverting anything; they're not getting any system or premise of a thing and upending it.

When I asked her about the ways action, contemplation, and rest intersect, Alicia replied:

I think this is where race enters into the conversation for me, as a Black woman. I think about who is afforded the space for rest and contemplation, and why it's so necessary to make room in the contemplative world and the temple of life for Black folks, Indigenous folks, and people of color. There are practices that I think we need to consider to be contemplative, but because they don't "fit" within the framework of whatever white contemplative spaces say makes sense, they get rejected or minimized or looked past. Given the demands that the world has on all of us as people of color, we're not always afforded the ability to be still. And stillness even means not having to be hyper-aware. And I think that that is a very important thing to think about, where we've seen shootings and police brutality impact people of color disproportionately. There's a state of hyper-awareness that I think contemplative practice can help us with. I know contemplative practice has helped me in calming my body. Doing some breath work has helped to lessen some of the anxiety that I felt in hearing and holding the things for folks who are impacted directly and also secondarily.

What could contemplative practice be like in this moment for those of us who are racially maligned and marginalized and oppressed around the world and in the US? Right now there's so much anxiety, there's so much anger, there's so much fear, even apathy. And I think that contemplative practice has the ability to take us out of those places—not out of them for the sake of bypassing them but for the sake of figuring out what we need in order to be well. Rest is one of those things. But how can you rest when shootings are affecting your community? How do you rest when the police beat a man to death? How do you rest? And I don't think that that's something that white contemplatives think about, in part because they're not even talking about these things. But we hold them, and that's why we can't rest.

2 | LIMITLESS EXPANSE
Queering the Monastery

> Queering requires that all boundaries be challenged, even those of sexual/gender definition. . . . The queer Christian body is a transgressive signifier of radical equality. . . . The queer body is any body.
> —Lisa Isherwood, "Queering Christ: Outrageous Acts and Theological Rebellions"

Queerness is antithetical to conformity. Monasticism's nonconformity to the world, in forgoing the typical way of doing life, is just one aspect that makes it queer. Monasteries became for me a place of my own queer emergence. In these strange spaces, I started to recognize the uniqueness I brought through my bodily presence. I began to notice the ways my queer body created a fecundity of limitless expanse just by showing up—not only at the monastery but in everyday life. With the companionship of queerness, my journey into the monastery became a kind of mirror to my own inward exploration. I began to live my life and truth in greater depth of liberation because the monastery reminded me of my own innate strangeness and profound power.

The monastery wasn't just a place for my silent, more introverted self. It wasn't just a place to bathe in the silence. It was a place for my most powerful and queer self. It was a place of my own becoming.

TRUST-FALLING INTO MYSELF

While organizing my mess of a desk recently, I saw this question scrawled on a piece of paper in the "to shred or not to shred" pile:

What would happen if *you* just welcomed *you*?

Clueless about what it was from and why it was there, I took a pause amid the organizing. While sitting with the phrase, I traced back the ways my sense of not feeling welcome, of not belonging, had been tethered to my experience of anxiety. I always held myself at arm's length—with the sense of not being good enough, confident enough, not the right body type, not intelligent enough—and thus, I often didn't welcome myself or feel comfortable in any given space.

These days, I have a much deeper understanding of my innate belonging, but the anxiety is still there. Now that I am more aware of my interconnectedness with all things—more enmeshed with the countless needs of my community and the world at large, the natural world's pain, and the suffering surrounding me—the anxiety has made a new home in my body.

Author Andrew Solomon once described his anxiety and panic disorder in a TED Talk in a way that made sense to me. "It was the feeling all the time like that feeling you have if you're walking and you slip or trip and the ground is rushing up at you, but instead of lasting half a second, the way that does, it lasted for six months," he said. "It's a sensation of being afraid all the time but not even knowing what it is that you're afraid of."

My first panic attack occurred in 2011 in the midst of a workday as a substance abuse counselor in Iowa. I was new to the field, overworked but doing the best I could, and my body just couldn't keep up. Facing the daily battles of the broken health-care system exhausted me. Paperwork piled up. All I really cared about were the life-changing interactions I was having with individual clients. Together we were going beyond the curriculum of the program to engage poets and thoughts disentangled from the rigidity forced upon us. At the same time, in my personal life I was in the midst of a dead-end relationship riddled with internalized patriarchy and homophobia—a relationship where welcomeness and belonging were only found in stolen and hidden moments. It's no wonder my body had had enough and finally put up the stop sign.

The day after my panic attack, I went back to work, grateful for the colleagues who had covered the rest of my shift, called to cancel my clients, and even run my intensive outpatient group that night. But at my desk that first day back, between clients, I eagerly continued reading the work of writers and poets—words inviting me into a new welcomeness, one of expanse and possibility, one where there was breathing room to be myself.

In the heightened fragility of having just moved through panic, my eyes kept hovering over a Merton essay titled "Integrity," which focused on what it might mean if I took a trust-fall into welcoming myself. "Many poets are not poets for the same reason that many religious men are not saints: *they never succeed in being themselves*," Merton writes. "They never get around to being the particular poet or the particular monk they are intended to be by God. They never become the [person] or the artist who is called for by all the circumstances of their individual lives. They waste their years in vain effort to be some other poet, some other saint."

These words rang in my soul like a bell of intuition, calling me closer to myself. They invited me into the depth of welcome of my own being, though I didn't know exactly what that meant at the time. The only thing I did know was that the stop sign of my body wasn't letting up and that pushing the brakes was the only option I had.

Pondering the options from my desk, I wondered what Merton, a cis white male immigrant from France, could teach me about myself. Tangled in this confusion and the delicate sensitivity of having just emerged from my first experience with panic, I wondered what I could learn from the location where these words were written—was it possible there was a spaciousness there that might invite me into welcoming myself more deeply?

Between clients that day, I had multiple browser tabs open to research monasteries and monastic life: *Who is Thomas Merton? What is the distance to Gethsemani Abbey, where he lived as a monk and hermit from 1915 until his death in 1968? Are there guest rooms?* Maybe it was a long shot for me (a woman, not Catholic, queer), but I still sent out an email in hopes of some reply.

To my surprise, within the day I received a response of warmth and hospitality. Immediately, I booked the next weekend available and then placed my request for time off to make the eleven-hour drive each way. Unbeknown to me, my journey of pausing to deeply welcome my own self was just beginning to unfold.

STRANGELY SPACIOUS BELONGING

The novelty of my weekend retreat at the monastery was as ignorant as it was adventurous. I arrived on a Friday, didn't think about what I would do, and didn't even think much about why I was there. I only knew to bring my pain and panic to this figurative altar of silence.

Having minimal knowledge of these monks and the sacred spaces they lived in, I was filled with curiosity about the history, sacredness, and seeming oddity of the monastic space. When I stepped into the empty church at Gethsemani Abbey, my ears tingled with the silence of nothingness. The monastery, founded in 1848, held an aura of mystery, a smell of frankincense and myrrh, and an eerie sense of knowing amid all the unknowns of my own life and of life at large. Aimlessly, I wandered the monastery grounds almost like I would a museum: a place to see monks as if they were some sort of monument to religion or life.

But not all feelings of history are comforting—in some monastic spaces and even particular rooms, I've also felt the uncomfortable sensation that *something bad happened here.* Or *something in this place doesn't offer me safety or welcome.* Given the abuse that has occurred in some monastic spaces, it's no wonder this feeling arose.

I joined the monks in their times of prayer: seven times a day, though the 3:30 a.m. bell was a bit early for me and the no-sleep nausea sent me promptly back to bed. In the prayers I did attend, however, some kind of trancelike peace washed over me. After the final prayer of the day, compline (from the Latin *completo- rium,* meaning "completion," representing the completion of the day), the monks at Gethsemani enter into total silence until the following day after Mass. The Church of England's website suggests that compline is most impactful when "the ending is indeed an ending, without additions, conversation or noise."

The silence became for me an emptiness, a steadiness, a solitude, a sacred pause, and a container of nothingness I could bathe in. Though at times the silence stirred me with the anxiety I was leaving behind, it was an informative anxiety, one telling my body to be, to center itself and listen to the nothingness. I came to experience the silence of the monastery as a deep respite. Silence was my place of rejuvenation, centering, and connecting to myself. Silence was a loving home for me to move freely within. Though I was the only one who could give myself the invitation into welcomeness, the silence of the monastery helped me to hear it more clearly, allowed me to understand the depth of belonging that was already a part of me.

The next day I visited the monastery's heritage center, where I read about the origin of the Trappists, also known as the Order of the Cistercians of the Strict Observance, in France in 1098 and gained insight into the monks' daily rhythm of *ora et labora* (Latin for "prayer and work"). I quickly became curious about this sacred pattern, this contemplative life bathed in solitude and silence.

But amid my pleasure, I also kept bumping into tensions. How can I feel such spaciousness in a place that requires the vows of fidelity to monastic life (often referred to as "conversion of manners/life"), obedience, stability (commitment to reside at the monastery), and even celibacy? Is it possible to find genuine safety in a space that doesn't "allow" for things like sexual expression (nor welcome my own as a queer woman in a Roman

Catholic institution)? Can I really revere a space that seems to honor contemplation over action and not hold them in union?

Why is it, I wondered, *that despite (or because of) the panic that brought me here, I feel so alive within these tensions, paradoxes, and seeming restrictions? How can I truly welcome and gather my full self here, in the submersion of silence, to emerge more authentically myself?*

From this strange place of curiosity, frustration, and aliveness, I wandered down the hallway to the guest master's office. "I love it here," I told him, "and I don't know why. Is it possible to stay one more night?"

With a softened face, he mumbled something under his breath, took out a pencil, and went over the calendar on his desk to see if an additional night were possible.

"I just can't get enough of this silence," I told him.

He found space for me to stay.

The next day, before packing up my car, I went back to the heritage center to study more about the monastic life and saw a map on the wall of seventeen Trappist monasteries in the United States. I noticed there was another monastery practically in my backyard, in Iowa. For a moment I thought wildly, *Perhaps I can visit all these monasteries and bathe in each of their silences.* Recognizing the impossibility of such a feat amid my career, I restrained my imagination. Even so, I snapped a photo of the map before making my way home.

For the eleven-hour drive back to Iowa, I remained still. Without reaching for the knob of the radio or the podcasts on my phone, I continued to feel submerged in that bath of silence and solitude that had brought my rattling, anxious soul back into alignment. It seemed I processed everything and nothing all at once in the quiet of the car. I gathered myself while letting myself be free. I found and welcomed myself anew. I was beginning to learn my own belonging.

Returning to my job the next day, I found that everything had changed. I knew whatever it was I had gotten in touch with at that monastery was a piece of the Divine and myself—a piece I was determined to chase after for the rest of my life. The Divine within the silence, the Divine of solitude and contemplation, the Divine of infinite expanse in the moments of mystery, the Divine who makes me laugh and cry with bafflement in the solitude of my own heart, the Divine who points me to more of myself in the infinite spaciousness of silence.

Days passed, and I caught myself sinking back into the same old anxious patterns of overwork and lack of self-care. I continued to yearn for that part of the Divine and myself I had met in the seemingly limitless walls of the monastery. Other than my individual work with clients, my job felt lifeless. I was getting restless for what I had experienced at Gethsemani. So, much like the day I began researching Thomas Merton and monasteries between clients, I began planning trips to the other monasteries I had seen on that map at the abbey.

I emailed nearly every one of those monasteries that day, asking about their availability and whether they welcomed guests for personal retreats. It became evident that I could plan these trips in a perfect order, following a route on the map and spaced out over about half a year. Realizing that my wild fantasy was a possibility, I checked and double-checked my savings account. And I knew without hesitation that it was time for me to put in my thirty-day notice at work and travel to all seventeen of these sacred spaces. It was time for me to bathe in these silences of rejuvenation, to take a journey into deepening my welcomeness and belonging.

And that's what I did.

Amid my planning, I prepared to meet with monks and nuns to discuss with them silence, solitude, and contemplative life. What I'd later learn is that they're *all* called monks or monastics, as "monk" comes from the Greek *monos*, meaning "alone." But as we know, society likes to create separations and binaries of everything, so the word for nuns comes from the Latin *nonnus*, meaning "monk."

Convincing my open-minded family that this was not about becoming a monk or a nun made for a fun conversation of its own! But luckily, coming from a family of creatives lends itself to making sense of these weird kinds of callings. I had no idea what I was doing, but I sure as hell knew I needed to do it.

Here was my plan: Beginning in 2012 and into 2013, I'd travel to all seventeen Trappist monasteries in the US. I'd bathe in their silences, have conversations with monks, and connect with the limitless expanse of my own self within the bounds of the monastery walls. I would deepen my own welcome and belonging by diving deep into spaces where I didn't quite fit. Queer as it may seem, it all made sense at the time.

I also began connecting the ways monastic life inhabits queerness of its own. I started to see its oddity in community living based on *The Rule of St. Benedict* from 530 CE (not all monastic orders are Benedictine, but those that are follow *The Rule*), strangeness in lives of silence and contemplation, and altogether queer way of life amid a world of discourse and chaos. I found that the queerness of monastic life informed my own queerness, revealing the limitless expanse in the queerness of my body and the monastery walls.

Though I've never thought of queerness as a container, the monastery began to show me the ways a container can infinitely expand in depth and height—the ways my soul, stilled and centered, can be a place of endless welcome and continual becoming. Queerness, I've found, is strangely specific and poetically free.

At the time, however, I didn't realize just how enmeshed this journey would become with my own queerness. I had yet to see the ways the monastic experience enlivened and strangely empowered my queerness. On the journey, I would begin to learn that my queerness longed for a spaciousness for its existence and evolution. As Black Canadian poet Brandon Wint wrote, "Not Queer like gay. Queer like, escaping definition. Queer like some sort of fluidity and limitlessness at once. Queer like a freedom too strange to be conquered. Queer like the fearlessness to imagine what love can look like . . . and pursue it."

My queerness resonated with these lessons from the monastic life: revelation lives in paradox; understanding, as opposed to knowing, thrives in unknowing; and welcomeness and belonging thrive in my continual becoming.

MONASTIC QUEERNESS

Why did the monastery become one of the places of my own queer emergence? The more I began to read about monastic life, the more I saw that something I had intuited was also being revealed. I was sinking my body into its own deep belonging. I was welcoming my true self in the silences of the spaces.

This expansion of self didn't lead to answers but to new questions. While at the beginning of the journey I was asking monks about silence, solitude, and contemplative life, by the end I was wondering about sexuality, self-expression, mental health, creativity, the difficulties in silence, and encounters with loneliness. I had begun asking: *Where does action fit into the contemplative life? How can a funneled focus cultivate an infinite depth? And how can we carry mystery and unknowing in everyday life?*

My queer body continued to push up against the notion that going away from the world was a way to love it more deeply. Amid my own understanding of the oppressions and injustices in the world, I found it hard to fathom that *this* particular path, this monastic way of life, was one of true balance. I could grasp silence and stillness as a means of convening with the Divine, but the lack of action *in* the world really stung.

Years later, I'd learn more about how monastics navigate this tension of contemplation and action. In 2021, I spoke with eighty-three-year-old Sister Barbara Jean LaRochester, a Black nun in the Carmelite order who shared that her camaraderie with the world amid the Black Lives Matter protests is founded in her patient endurance:

What happens with me is the pain that I feel that's the patient endurance. And that becomes a prayer: *God, I can't be out there to walk, I can't be there to express what I would like to say even to help. But I ask you to use the pain that I'm feeling.* Patient endurance is individual, it's communal, and the people that are going through this—they are out there, but they are doing this every day. I am the same way, but I am inside and

I am going through it with them. They were on the front lines, and I feel the pain.

This monastic way of intervening for and with the pain of the world is no doubt queer. It's an angle of communion and connection that subverts norms and the typical way of doing things. And it also sparks my imagination to think of the ways my own energy—in silence, in prayer—might also queerly engage with those in pain I may not be able to reach. Not as a means to avoid action, but as a way to engage more fully with the pain of the world.

Like queerness, monasticism persists and continues to endure. And the queerness of the monastery is as old as the queerness of Christianity. Examples of monastic queerness live in the stories of people like Pelagia, a sex worker turned hermit monk who lived out his days in fourth- or fifth-century Antioch as a trans man. And Walatta Petros, a nun in seventeenth-century Ethiopia who is said to have fallen in love with fellow nun Eheta Kristos. Lesbian author Kittredge Cherry cultivated an entire website (qspirit.net) dedicated to telling the stories of the queer monastics, saints, and Christians among us, including individuals, couples, and a story about Saint Matrona of Perge, who founded a convent where nuns dressed as men in fifth-century Constantinople.

THE QUEER MONASTIC WELCOME

It's been over ten years since I quit my job to travel to the seventeen Trappist monasteries, but the silences still astonish me. The silence still beckons me, like the prairie land behind my childhood home did. But now that the novelty has worn off, I know exactly what to expect. The monastic silence will still me until I hear the voice and pain within myself and the world, to welcome more of myself and those around me, to understand more about my—and all of our—belonging.

A few months ago, I traveled to a nearby monastery for a time of reconnecting with the limitless expanse I always seemed to find there. Much like other monasteries I had been to, this Episcopal Benedictine abbey hosted the same rhythms of prayer by following the Liturgy of the Hours, praying seven times a day. But at this monastery, things felt and looked slightly different. Though the Episcopal church has its own set of deeply entrenched institutional violence, there is less-rigid hierarchical authority, greater inclusivity of women and queer priests, and no eucharistic gatekeeping. In fact, when I pulled out the "Q" card-catalog slot in the abbey's library, I found more than ten books with "Queer" in the title. That didn't even include the two dozen or so books on LGBTQIA+ thoughts, ideas, and stories. Here, my first conversations with the guest master were about a local lesbian Episcopal priest who regularly visits with her wife.

While I've found the monastery to be a space where my queerness is engaged and my whole self is welcomed, I recognize that it's not a place for everyone. Not only is Christian monastic life in America predominantly white, but many monasteries I've been to are also Roman Catholic. I have had conversations with monks and priests about their individual affirming stances—and of course my "queerdar" has gone off plenty of times in the Catholic monastery. But in a very real sense all of them are *not* affirming, by nature of their connection to the institutional violence of the Catholic church (via oppression of LGBTQIA+

folks, Indigenous folks, people of color, violence toward children, and oppression of women).

For those of us who identify as queer or seek queer spaces in solidarity with the LGBTQIA+ community, there are plenty of other options to soak in this limitless expanse, this infinite silence, without being in fear of danger or harm to mind, body, or soul. And that is precisely what queer—and all marginalized folks—deserve: a place of rest and respite, a place of expansiveness and welcome without fear. Whether that sacred space is the home altar, the inner sanctuary, or a monastery, it doesn't matter. What matters is that welcomeness and belonging live in moments and places of spaciousness. What matters is that we tilt our heads to queerly look at the sliver of time we have and bathe deeply in the waters that we find to be healing, submerging ourselves in the truth of our welcome.

Going away from the world in order to love it more deeply is indeed a privilege. The ability to even access a monastery is a privilege: tapping into a savings account, taking time off, for some of us finding childcare, traveling. But when we queerly shift the way we think about monastic retreats, we can begin to travel within our own bodies to the places where the queerness of the monastery is mimicked. The *inward* monastery—the inward hermitage, the silent space away, whatever we want to call it—is the place within ourselves of our deepest welcome, our clearest belonging. Here, in the monastery of our own being, we can learn to name the seconds, minutes, and hours of everyday life as places of welcomeness, belonging, respite, refreshment, and connection to self, the Divine, and others.

We must queer or eschew dominative structures so the contemplative heart is not one that retreats from required actions in the world. Perhaps the monastic life can be a daily rhythm, cultivated in our everyday experience. Perhaps queerness has more to teach us about this daily rhythm than we could imagine. Perhaps queerness itself is an invitation into the limitless expanse of oneself and one's contemplative expressions. As I read Howard Thurman, I meet something that brings together the idea of a monastery within, where clarity is distilled for everyday action. "I determine to live the outer life in the inward sanctuary," Thurman writes. "The outer life must find its meaning, the source of its strength in the inward sanctuary. As this is done, the gulf between outer and inner will narrow and my life will be increasingly whole and of one piece. What I do in the outer will be blessed by the holiness of the inward sanctuary; for indeed it shall all be one."

AN INVITATION TO QUEER THE MONASTERY

Rev. Jes Kast (she/her/hers)

This interview for the *Queering Contemplation* podcast took place March 20, 2023, on Zoom.

I first came across the work of Rev. Jes Kast on social media. Once a pastor at a United Church of Christ church in New York City, mingling with friends like Tim Gunn, she now lives with her wife in Pennsylvania, where they enjoy the slow grounding of cultivating home. There, she focuses on their vegetable garden, their dog, and living into what it means to be a community. A consistent theme in Jes's work is her frequent visits to monasteries for respite and rest, naming her times there "nun camp." There, she finds something in the sacred rhythm of the monastery that can't be found anywhere else. What I love about Rev. Jes's story is that it is rich with personal experience, a love of nuns, liturgy, and a fabulous queerness—all of which she takes with her into the monastic spaces she visits:

I love nuns so much. My friend and brother, Matt, who is a Jesuit brother, always says, "This is Pastor Jes, friend of nuns."

The defining moment of when I began to very much be called into monastic spaces was when I was a first-year student in seminary. And during that first January, when you have interesting class experiences, we went to a monastery in the Midwest for two nights and three days. My best friend at the time was Rachel, and she and I called it "nun camp." And that's kind of stuck with my language because even in my congregation, people know, *Pastor Jes is going to nun camp.*

I remember we didn't have to get up in the morning and go to prayers at the monastery; we had our own structured retreat. But I really wanted to go. And I don't remember the name of the sister, but she shared the prayer book with me and we sat together. I just love these older women: these strong matriarchs who have lived such incredibly interesting lives being in such a feminine, spiritual, powerful place. I felt nurtured and held and a sense of belonging.

And since then, as I've come out and identify as a queer person, I have found different monastic communities that are pretty queer in themselves. The idea that I'm queer is only one interesting aspect about me—there are many other interesting aspects about me, which feels really good. And I have found these ecologically aware and environmental nuns in Loretto, Kentucky, and Erie, Pennsylvania, and I love the intentional space of: *We're going to be still together. That's how we're going to be. That's how we're going to get to know each other; we're going to just sit together in quiet.* Oh my gosh, it's so awesome! I love it so much! Particularly as a Protestant minister, where words are a thing, I find it powerful to just be intimate and be known in silence. Really powerful and intimate, and really freakin' queer—*We're going to sit together for thirty minutes in this circle and just be quiet.* That's really queer. You live so close to those people and then you just go to lunch, and wow, look at this connection we've just created. That's really queer to me.

3 | INFINITE POSSIBILITY
Queering Silence

> If we pursue silence wholeheartedly, what we are left
> with in the end is ourselves and a curiosity about the
> essence of being in the world. . . . Silence marks the birth
> and death of all our fragile attempts to grasp at mystery.
>   —Patrick Shen, *Notes on Silence*

"Is it okay to hold your hand?"

I was at dinner with the woman I had been dating for several
years, but these questions had become routine. She wasn't out
yet, and I was never sure how much I had to hide our being
together.

"I might know someone here," she said. It had become
another way to remind me not to show physical affection in public
places. I became accustomed to accepting the breadcrumbs of a
kiss in the musty garage or a lingering hug after everyone finally
fell asleep when we were visiting her childhood home and were
relegated to separate beds.

Other than a few close friends willing to keep a secret, until
eventually some less-feared family members were chosen to be
included, nobody in her life knew we were more than friends. I
was a secret, and I was a part of the silence-keeping that secret
required.

For over five years, I actively participated in one of the most toxic silences of my life. I was in a romantic relationship with someone who wouldn't publicly date me because they weren't open about their sexuality. At the mercy of someone else's comfort—or lack thereof—I participated in a silencing of myself in public places, around family members, with friends, at work, even at the grocery store. This added to the years of yielding to internalized patriarchy and heteronormativity's grasp on my life—years I'd never regain. This kind of silence, brought on by shame, creates long-lasting damage and knots to be untied for years to come. Silence where love cannot prevail is a place of toxicity, a place of stunted existence.

Years later, when the relationship finally ended, I vowed never again to sacrifice myself on the altar of someone else's self-discovery. I would never again silence the fullness of my truest self for another's comfort.

These kinds of silences had become a part of my natural milieu while I was growing up as a queer kid: silencing myself by not expressing a crush, hushing my feelings and emotions, quieting myself by not realizing that queerness was even an option, and even dampening the queerness of myself and others with shame-filled "come to Jesus" letters. One of the most mortifying ways I participated in this toxic and often violent silence was during the fundamentalist evangelical era of my life, when I attended an Exodus International conference under the guise of "helping" a queer person in my own life. This organization, which sought to change people with "same-sex attraction," finally closed in 2013. But before it did, many queer folks endured trauma and harm through the organization's focus on "conversion therapy," a so-called therapy proven to be violent to LGBTQIA+ people and renounced by count-less psychology and counseling boards across America. Never in my life to that point had I been in the company of so many other queer folks as I was at that conference. Never since have I been in the presence of so many queer folks filled with so much shame, caused by the perpetuated falsities and violence of religious interpretation.

Thankfully, toxic silences can be transformed into action. An example of this comes from the late 1980s, amid the toxic silence of the LGBTQIA+ community and the world at large during the AIDS epidemic. During this time, the organization ACT UP (AIDS Coalition To Unleash Power) was founded alongside the slogan "Silence = Death." The organization's work led to greater access to testing, medicine, and medical care for those navigating the AIDS crisis. As many queer folks have shown us throughout the years, these activists pointed directly to the ways toxic silence perpetuated death and demanded something different.

Toxic silence and silencing don't just exist in the area of LGBTQIA+ issues, of course. For centuries people of color, women, the disabled community, and others have been silenced because they disrupt the status quo and shake the foundations of perceived reality. Meanwhile, these marginalized groups are almost always pointing us to where the truth resides, where reality is unveiled, where interdependence and communal care must exist for the liberation of all people. And I am not exempt. I've also been part of this toxic silencing. In a number of situations, I've failed to speak up when there's been opposition or lack of understanding about the humanity and dignity of someone. In many ways, toxic silence has a grasp on us all. It often floods us with shame and then silences our truest intuition. It is the sliver of fear that rises within us when encountering something of ourselves or others we don't yet understand.

Parsing out the distinctions between toxic silence and loving silence is important. We need to name toxic silence as the silence that causes harm, shame, minimization, and damage to our world. And we need to name loving silence as the silence that is generative and creative, a silence that deepens our unity with self and others—the kind of silence that cultivates a more expansive and loving world.

At first glance, this may seem to set up a binary of "good" and "bad" silence. But on the contrary, silence's spectrum of existence can work its way queerly into our lives, creating a variety of results and encounters, or none at all. Silence is a paradox in this way, because every effort to discuss it ends up dissolving it. And paradox is profoundly queer, while also being the precise place in which spiritual life flourishes.

When I finally stepped away from that relationship's hamster wheel of toxic silence, I began to see how I had silenced other parts of myself. Beyond the ways I was hiding my sexuality, I also hid parts of myself informed by intuition—places of creativity and aliveness, places of openness and community, places of clarity and calm—ultimately the places where a loving silence thrived. As I yielded to the vacuum of toxic silence the relationship required for its survival, the air was also sucked out of my evolution of identity, self-expression, and unique way of being.

Now, amid the full embrace of my own queerness, I use my voice when my intuition beckons. Engaging my queerness has disrupted the systems that constrain me—even systems I internalize. Queerness demands I move through my discomfort to speak out and speak up for myself and those around me. In my voicing of queerness, and in naming the fact that I am queer, I find myself standing not only *for* who I am, but also *against* the constraints of limits. Womanist theologian Rev. Dr. Pamela Lightsey suggests that queerness is "not only my self-identity; it is also my active engagement against heteronormativity." Voicing queerness has allowed me to more quickly recognize my own silent acceptance of patriarchy, the subliminal disguise of heteronormativity, hidden Eurocentricity, and internalized capitalistic views that move me away from interdependence. The queer part of me disrupts the silence of shame and allows me to be boldly against the things that sideline the fullness and truth of myself and my fellow humans.

In the Christian context, the toxicity of silent bystanders creates and feeds countless acts of violence: the sexual abuse in many church settings and its continuation through empty apologies; Christianity's lack of reckoning with its history of colonization; denominations' refusal to honor and elevate the leadership and dignity of women, people of color, refugees, people with disabilities, and people from other marginalized communities; churches filling with Christian nationalism and white supremacy culture; the countless times the silent acceptance of bad theology has caused an LGBTQIA+ person to hate or harm themselves; and more. This is the silence of harm, violence, shame, and toxicity.

Contemplative silence, on the other hand, *can* be a loving silence, but it too comes to us dragging its long list of failures, including the times it failed to speak up, the moments it was not tethered to action, times it was led by a teacher or practitioner who caused harm, and anytime it chose to opt out while witnessing injustice. Contemplative silence, in the form of a practice, provides a place where a loving silence *can* be formed and found, but not when it is used as a place to hide from ourselves, our loved ones, or our communities. Because when contemplative silence is used as a protective layer, diminishing loving presence and action, it damages the beauty of silence and can become harmful.

Toxic silence is embedded in the fabric of our daily lives. It lives in systems that may be internalized or clearly seen. Yet a loving silence can also be pursued, and we can seek and find it even in the chaos of our days. Sometimes it seeps in with our efforts to repeat an internal mantra or take an intentional pause, at other times it pours in like the colorful morning light through the east-facing window. This is the contemplative silence I continually seek and practice. This silence regenerates, regulates, and allows for the emergence of loving presence and action. The more we engage in the silences that *aren't* toxic—the beautiful, loving, and infinite possibilities of silence—the more we encounter silence as a creative, generative force and not a destructive one.

MORNING LIGHT LOVER

Loving silence first poured through my windows early on in life. When I was about eight years old, I would wander behind my childhood home and into a vast landscape of prairie grasses no more than a quarter mile away. There I would look up, bask in the Iowa sky, breathe, and usually cry. If you've ever been to the Midwest, you may have been disenchanted by its flatness, but looking up, you can almost always see an ocean of blue.

Growing up in this landscape on the edge of town carried some challenges, like being far away from friends, but the value of being able to walk into the prairie as my big emotions began to stir was a gift that far outweighed any challenges. This little introvert secretly loved the solitude that distance provided; a solitude that I found deepened my love of others. Indoors, I'd begin to feel my big feelings and not have clarity on how to direct or process them. Then I'd go outside into the loving presence of the prairie and move through them in the boundless container of silence's landscape. This pursuit of a loving silence became a part of my routine, a regular practice. And this movement—embodying my emotions to better understand and metabolize them—helped the clouds lift for a clearer understanding of myself. I'd walk back to the prairie, usually feeling emotions like anger or fear, and then lie down and look up at the infinite spaciousness of the sky. I'd move into the deeper reality of my underlying feelings, revealing sadness or hurt. Under this sky, there was infinite possibility. Under this sky, I was captivated as though by a horizonless ocean. Under this sky, I recognized a landscape mimicking my own interior self and discovered a patchwork of possibilities.

I didn't know it, but my eight-year-old self was taking notes from the sixth-century monks of Iona. On their little Scottish isle surrounded by the sea, the monks would imagine the sea as a desert. They would enter into a space of imagination to engage the "opposite" element, trading sea for sand, while longing for the same emptiness and silence their ancestral desert dwellers of third- and fourth-century Christianity experienced. They cultivated this image of a metaphorical desert to journey into the unknown and open themselves up to trusting the Divine. The landscapes of silence they explored to mimic the interior self were vistas not only relegated to the realm of spirituality but essential to life.

Today, my process of moving through emotions hasn't changed much. I continue to go to my inner world, or my interior monastery, to better understand myself. And I still pursue the silence within moments of big emotions. I no longer live near the prairie, so the sky's vastness is harder to find. Now, the constant hum of traffic and buzz of everyday life encroaches on my senses, and it takes more effort to move into that infinite spaciousness of the silent landscapes, even as it remains a worthy endeavor. I've come to realize that the imagination can do marvelous things even in the smallest of natural spaces. Taking notes from the monks of Iona, a lake can become an ocean, a tree can be a forest, and even a stone can become a mountain. In these natural places, silence speaks, especially within its emptiness. She offers us a sense of sorting that calls forth our deepest instincts, inviting us into the best parts of ourselves.

Often, to meet this vastness in shortened moments or loud spaces, I seek silence's landscape. To do that, I repeat a mantra of sorts: "Carry the silence and stillness within." I remind myself that my body can be a vessel of that vast silent landscape. As I carry the silence and stillness within, I am reminded of that infinite blank canvas of the Iowa sky or the unending waves of the Pacific Ocean. We can create these moments of silence any time we make the choice to step outside the chaos of the room, to linger in the tender pause with our beloved, or to soften our gaze while looking out the window. In this silence, queered by the imagination and armed with infinite possibility, we can find the spaciousness to become, to wholly engage with ourselves and others, and to consider our deepest longings.

Because the queerness of silence exists in its connectivity to infinite possibility—the infinite possibility of love *and* life—I understand that my pursuit of silence has also been a pursuit and unveiling of my own queerness. Silence itself is already innately queer in its ambiguity and possibility. Silence pushes beyond binaries and spectrums of existence. Each time we are tempted to describe silence as everywhere and nowhere, as a safe embrace and open hands, silence reminds us that its thriving only resides in its paradox of existence; its truth is in its potency of indescribability. Silence, as a monk once told me, "is the tomb of Christ. It is the place of infinite possibility."

So, over the last ten years, even when flotsam from the toxicity of that silencing relationship arose, I began to recognize the ways loving silence would also emerge and greet me softly. I took notice of the loving silence in my times alone, in the monasteries I visited, on my hikes, and in my creativity. Loving silence invited me into my own becoming and queerness. As I accepted the invitation, I saw more clearly what I had determinedly, albeit sometimes unknowingly, chased my entire life—the transcendent nature of silence, those aspects I knew to be beautiful and enduring: the Divine found in its spaciousness, and its unending permission and creativity to be exactly who I am.

In 2014, I began working on the production team of the documentary film *In Pursuit of Silence* with director Patrick Shen, and later started cohosting the *Encountering Silence* podcast with Kevin Johnson and Carl McColman. While these were all expressions of loving silence, it wasn't cultivated in the *doing* of my life; it was only in the moments of *being*. By remaining in this loving silence, I carved out a new ethic: one of love, openhandedness, curiosity, and care. This silence not only revealed its innate queerness by so lovingly holding possibility; it also became for me a harbor of clarity.

Practicing loving silence takes the time and effort of listening to something from the quietest parts of ourselves. And that listening is not always easy. Many times, we go into loving silence only to find our minds stirring with everything from the dreadful sorrows of our lives to the to-do lists of our day. Sometimes this silence is too difficult to sit within, or we find ourselves moved to unknown tears; other times the silence is so empty we feel utterly alone. In these moments, silence challenges us to heal, grow, learn, and lean deeper into the depths of love. In these moments, silence remains loving in its spacious, yet grounded, way of being.

I've often described this loving silence visually, as a silence that grounds and roots me deeply into the soil of nutrients so I am able to connect to, understand, and love my own roots and those roots nearby. Only here, amid this loving silence, can I see the possibilities before me: a vision for the depth of pathways in the soil below. Here—in the infinite vastness of the sky, in the horizonless ocean, in the heights beyond the clouds and the depths below the soil's surface—loving silence invites us into our own interior landscape, our own infinite possibility, our own queer existence.

SILENCE IS SPOKEN HERE

Loving silence in our interior life is accessible to all of us, no matter who we are or where we are. Yet even at this entrance into our deepest interior self, it's not always safe to meet the silence alone. Some of us need the support and safety of a therapist, the companionship of a group to practice with, our beloved partner, or a trusted confidant.

Silence in the form of formal practices, like structured meditation, can represent both expansive possibility and minimized accessibility. Whether intentionally or not, teachers and designers of formal practices of silence can create systems of dominance and inadvertently or directly restrict access. The practice I am most familiar with in the Christian contemplative tradition is centering prayer, which comes from the late Thomas Keating (1923–2018). Keating, a Trappist monk at St. Benedict's Monastery in Snowmass, Colorado, was well known for saying, "Silence is God's first language; everything else is a poor translation." The prayer practice takes place in four steps: selecting a sacred word, sitting comfortably with one's eyes closed while introducing the sacred word mentally, continually guiding oneself back to the word, and sitting in silence for a couple of minutes after the silent prayer. A minimum of twenty minutes is suggested.

Although I've found practices like this helpful, I also wonder: If silence is perpetually contained so that we might get a taste of its beauty, how can the fullness of loving silence emerge—its infinite possibility and therefore queerest expression? *Maybe*, I answer myself, *loving silence only exists in the untamed wildness.* Maybe it is only when the magic of the sky above us becomes an ocean or the rock on our altar reveals to us a mountain. Maybe silence is its most loving and alive self only when we surrender to its emptiness.

After visiting St. Benedict's Monastery, and while traveling to other monasteries across America, I found myself engaging with a silent prayer practice of my own. During my visit to Our Lady of the Angels Monastery in Crozet, Virginia, I met with a nun I'll call Sister Nancy to discuss silence on a deeper level, detached from formalities and structured practices. Sister Nancy and I addressed the terror I encountered when sitting in silence for long periods of time. I had begun learning that the untamed spaciousness of silence, even during the formality of a practice, could be a place of danger, fear, or even harm. Simultaneously elated and horrified by the places this untamed silence would take me, I shared with her more about my experience. The silence had begun to expose parts of myself I didn't want to see, know, or hear. Nor did I feel equipped to meet those fears, which grew out of encountering the deep hatred and harm of which I'm capable. I began to recognize more clearly the importance of support—through a trusted companion, a group to practice with, a therapist, a spiritual director, or other resources—while diving into silence during more sensitive times in my life.

Silence speaks. And I often found—and still find—that silence breathes love and expanse into the corners of our bodily knowing, revealing the truth of ourselves to ourselves. Silence isn't always easy or simple, because silence reveals.

Sister Nancy told me that to understand the usefulness and accuracy of one's silence, "love is the great discernment." She taught me that silence needs its own spaciousness, its own weirdness, its own infinite possibility, to be fully alive. Loving silence cannot be tethered to secrets, silencing, or any of toxic silence's acts of violence. For the sake of discernment and survival, silence must be bound to love. Real love. Not secret love. Queer, unashamed love.

Loving silence is spacious. It reveals the truths of ourselves, invites us into infinite possibilities, and is a place of unfathomable paradox. Silence's innate queerness reminds us that our spiritual life flourishes in the places of paradox, the unknowns, and the imagination, for queerness invites loving silence to break barriers and expectations. Queerness invites us to hold this tension of silence with clarity, effectiveness, and action. Queerness and silence remind each other that they are places of infinite possibility—that *we* are places of infinite possibility.

AN INVITATION TO QUEER SILENCE

Dr. Kevin Quashie (he/him/his)

I first met Dr. Quashie over a virtual gathering for the *Encountering Silence* podcast. His presence was like the softness and warmth of a loving silence that seeps into a day without effort or intention. To say our time felt like a euphoric silent meditation sit would be an understatement. He shared about his work in Black cultural, Black literary, Black queer, and Black aesthetics studies at Brown University.

In his book *The Sovereignty of Quiet: Beyond Resistance in Black Culture*, Dr. Quashie discusses the differences between silence and quiet, and unpacks the podium image at the 1968 Summer Olympics in Mexico City, where United States sprinters Tommie Smith and John Carlos protested by raising their fists in silence:

> Silence often denotes something that is suppressed or repressed, and is an interiority that is about withholding, absence, and stillness. Quiet, on the other hand, is presence (one can, for example, describe prose or a sound as quiet) and can encompass fantastic motion. It is true that silence can be expressive, but its expression is often based on refusal or protest, not the abundance and wildness of

the interior described above. Indeed, the expressiveness of silence is often aware of an audience, a watcher or listener whose presence is the reason for the withholding—it is an expressiveness which is intent and even defiant. This is a key difference between the two terms because in its inwardness, the aesthetic of quiet is watcherless. . . .

An essential aspect to the idiom of prayer is waiting: the praying subject waits with agency, where waiting is not the result of having been acted upon (as in being made to wait), but is itself action. In waiting, there is no clear language or determined outcome; there is simply the practice of contemplation and discernment. This is a challenge to the way we commonly think of waiting, which is passive; it is also a disruption of the calculus of cause and effect which shapes so much of how we understand the social world. . . .

This idea that prayer can articulate beyond its own self-indulgence is important to thinking about the bowed heads of Tommie Smith and John Carlos; that is, to read their protest as quiet expressiveness does not disavow their capacity to inspire. In fact, nothing speaks more to their humanity—and against the violence of racism—than the glimpse of their inner lives. The challenge, though, is to understand how their quiet works as a public gesture, without disregarding its interiority.

4 | CONTINUAL TRANSCENDENCE
Queering Mysticism

Those words, *mysticism* and *contemplation*, seem spooky to people, but everybody can be a mystic. The root of mystic is *myst*, which is the same root in mystery. Mystic basically means that you're living with a certain amount of uncertainty, and whether we like it or not, we all have some uncertainty. The only difference between a contemplative or mystic and the "normal" person who might be living with uncertainty is that mystics embrace it.

—Therese Taylor-Stinson, *Contemplating Now* podcast

Mysticism is a threshold into divine enmeshment. Transcending all that is, mysticism leaves us wordless, breathless, and immersed in wonder. While mysticism might sound otherworldly—and it is, in a way—mystical encounters are also less rare than some think. "I think people have mystical experiences all the time," Dr. Lerita Coleman Brown, author of *What Makes You Come Alive: A Spiritual Walk with Howard Thurman*, said. "But we tend to think about mysticism as something sort of mysterious. . . . Mysticism is just one of those kinds of things that happens."

Queerness is an invitation into possibilities beyond what exists. So what might it look like to queer our entanglements with the Divine beyond what *is* for what *could be*? What if queering mysticism is an invitation into life beyond the status quo of the same old relationships with ourselves, others, and the Divine? What if we recognized mysticism's innate queerness as a means of accepting its vastness of existence in everyday life? What if mysticism is more accessible than we think?

Mysticism transcends boundaries, definitions, origins, and expectations. In this way, mysticism has been queer from the very beginning. Like queerness, mysticism cannot live in the false certitude of a definition, because it goes beyond knowing and unknowing. Definitions often fail us. They try to encapsulate something that cannot be boxed in. And mysticism calls into question the normativity of definitions that imply there are "acceptable" expressions or practices. Dorothee Sölle writes, "All mysticism is a part of the endeavor to escape from this fate of language that serves the exercise of power, control, and possession." And indeed, definitions are imprinted with the power of the institutions or systems from which they come. Dr. Joy R. Bostic writes that "along with gender, issues of race and economic status are also entangled in how definitions of mysticism are socially constructed."

Mysticism is a constant invitation into transcendence: a subversion of what causes harm, an awakening of ecstasy, eroticism, pleasure, play, and even protest, in the form of social-justice activism. Mysticism is our body's full engagement in acts that deepen our recognition of and connectivity to ourselves, each other, nature, and the Divine.

So if we cannot name or contain mysticism, *what is it?* Like creating a statue, perhaps we can carve out what it is *not*. Or maybe we can name what we *do* know it is tethered to.

The continual transcendence of mysticism is also a revolt against the things that claim and constrain us. We know mysticism is an enmeshment with the Divine in a way we cannot define, explain, or name. We know that the transcendence of mysticism often disrupts the status quo and any other dominating force that hinders liberation for all. This transcendence, as a part of mystical expression or encounter, is a way of prophetically seeing how liberation, love, and even joy, pleasure, and rest can be pursued.

Dorothee Sölle's words on mysticism could be interchanged with the work of an activist when she writes, "Mutual dependence is the fundamental model that mysticism has put in place of domination." And Rev. Dr. Barbara A. Holmes suggests that a public mystic is "a leader whose interiority and communal reference points must intersect." Does the transcendence a mystic reaches come from acts of interdependence, whether in solitude or on the streets of protest?

Though the mystical encounter may not always be an action, mysticism, like contemplation, also cannot be limited to inaction. In fact, Dr. Bostic writes that mysticism is authentic only when it is manifested in the world; mysticism's relationship to embodiment is a place of transformation and expression. What would happen if we queered our same old ways of understanding mysticism by opening ourselves up to these invitations of continual transcendence?

Christian mysticism has consistently been a place of belonging for misfits, outcasts, and weirdos—all of those who could not be contained by the bounds of normalcy. These mystics have fallen in love with trees, written love poems to the Divine, and voiced prophecy into movements of justice. Dr. Miguel H. Díaz says that the work of fourteenth-century mystic St. John of the Cross "opens the door for understanding not only the erotic elements of mystical experiences but also the mystical elements in erotic experiences." Mysticism, in its continual transcendence of definition, expression, and expectation, shows itself to be radically queer and ever evolving. And it invites us to join that continuance.

I KISSED A TREE, AND I LIKED IT

Similar to the ways contemplation and action have been enmeshed since time immemorial, eroticism and mysticism are partners, much as the mountain is covered in trees and the sea is proximal to the shore. While I can't recall the first time I felt that sense of electricity between myself and another person, I do know it wasn't until much later in life that my sexual desires and expressions were able to merge with my spirituality. That's something that the trees taught me and the seashore played out in front of me: waters enlivening, enveloping, and awakening the shore as the sands stirred within the water's rhythm. Now I regularly experience that intertwining of sexuality and spirituality and their constancy together.

Many mystics and contemplatives have written about their love of trees and natural places. Howard Thurman wrote about the oak tree he communed with: "The tree," he said, "would take out my bruises and my joys, unfold them, and talk about them." And Black queer poet and activist Davelyn Hill, while navigating illness and a new diagnosis, shared, "I had a tree outside my window, and I named the tree Dolores. . . . I would stare at Dolores, I would talk to Dolores. And Dolores got me through, just thinking about her roots."

In the early winter months of 2021, I knew I needed to reawaken this connectivity to the trees and mountains. So as soon as I could find some time in my work schedule, I took myself to the nearest mountain range. Saturated in solitude at the edge of the Great Smoky Mountains, I steeped myself in a time of rituals, pauses, fires, stream listening, slowness, hiking, and paying close attention to the ways natural beauty softens me. My jaw released, my shoulders softened, my eyes calmed, and the tenderness of my truest self showed up.

On my second day in the mountains, I wandered upon an empty trail and made my way up until a tree caught my eye. Like flirty eye contact from across the room, we kept catching each other. Then I finally worked up the courage to go closer. Slowly approaching her in all her sugar-maple beauty, I eventually put my hand on her chest as if to reach her heartbeat. Then I turned around and put my back up against hers. Sliding down her spine to the ground, I felt her trunk cup my back like a chair she made just for my body. *Just for me,* I thought. No matter that the ground was wet, I sensed a deep belonging. Elated by the moment with her, I basked in some kind of a romance taking place between us. She spoke to me the words of affirmation I had been reciting to myself in recent days, words I longed to hear from outside myself.

You are okay, she told me.

You are good enough, you are loved, you belong, she reminded me.

You will get through this. You will be okay.

Then, I felt her loving arms wrap around my waist as she whispered what I'd been needing most: *You are here, you are here, you are here.* My face immediately softened even more—in the way it only does when I'm in love, when I feel safe and vulnerable, when I feel at home, when I am stilled, when I remember to *be* instead of *do*. When I recall that being is enough. *I am enough* and *the moment is enough.*

For some time longer I sat with her, embraced by her, and in the silence, I listened longer. I softened deeper and deeper into her, feeling like I was falling into her roots of wisdom. Immersed in her silent witness of the world, I accepted her love, her boughs covering me like a blanket. I considered the pathways of her roots and branches binding her to other trees, to other life, to humanity, to me, to us. She taught me to breathe deeply again in that moment of romance. She led me into the mystical encounter of love, where borders dissolve and we can sense the truth of our interconnection.

Eventually, the trail called me back. I stood up. Bowed in gratitude. Hugged and kissed her goodbye. I kissed a tree, and I liked it.

Even as this wasn't my first mystical romance with a tree, it felt brand new. The timing was healing, and the relational reciprocity allowed me to return to myself once again. That day as I headed back down the path, having said goodbye to the tree, I felt entirely renewed. Our time together had reminded me that my love of nature and my connectivity to the world around me are sustaining. The love and connection with oneself and with another can always be reawakened, renewed, and deepened. I was reminded that mystical encounter is a particular rousing of my connection to the Divine; it is erotic in the ways it points to and deepens our mutual reliance, vulnerability, trust, and love.

Mysticism as a practice is unitive. It is also erotic in its reception, reciprocity, and expression. And if the undefinable mystical moment connects us to the erotically Divine within and around us, queerness invites us to see the ways the moment merges into unity. Queerness is the invitation to tilt our heads and see the moment's transcendence, the encounter's eroticism, the unitive expression—and to experience our interconnectedness.

THE INNER STANCE

In 2015, I was attending my first conference with the International Thomas Merton Society at Bellarmine University in Louisville, Kentucky. There I heard psychotherapist Dr. Jim Finley speak from the heart about his experience being a novice (a new monk) under the direction of Thomas Merton, and some of the many life lessons he's experienced since then. It was here that I first heard Jim describe the mystical experience of unity in love-making: a creative unfolding, encounter, and interconnection. "The poet cannot make the poem happen, but the poet can assume the inner stance that offers the least resistance to be overtaken by the gift of poetry," he said. "Those committed to healing cannot make healing happen, but they can assume the inner stance that offers the least resistance to the gift of healing. Lovers cannot make their moments of oceanic oneness happen, but together they can assume the stance that offers the least resistance to be overtaken one more time by the gift of oceanic oneness."

What might it mean for us to assume the particular inner stance that each moment invites us into? How might we queer the moment, queer our inner stance, by opening ourselves up to the countless possibilities of continual transcendence? How might it feel to meet the mystical in ourselves, nature, our beloved, and the Divine through this oceanic oneness?

When we are safe with our partner, creating immeasurable oneness in love-making, moments of sexual expression or exploration—we can experience our spirituality deeply enmeshed with embodiment and sexuality. Like creating a poem or being suddenly struck with awe, the mystical encounter in moments of eroticism is an expression—and also sometimes an explosion—of unity. It is relational, embracing, entwined, dancelike—and never forced.

Contemplation creates the momentum toward this unitive experience. As Evelyn Underhill said, "Contemplation is the mystic's medium." Contemplation moves us toward mystical encounter by reminding us to begin from a place of openness, creativity, curiosity, and interconnection. When we rest in the wisdom of our lover's eyes, when we keep the light on to look at them just a little bit longer, when we contemplate our overwhelming admiration for who they are, we begin to assume that inner stance. The moments we find ourselves in a timeless embrace, falling in love with a tree, creating oneness, or making art from divine entwinement—these moments of eroticism and mysticism are also places of perpetual awakening. When these encounters merge—like the tree and the mountain, the sea and the shore, the poet and the poem, the lovers in union—we feel more alive and in touch with all of creation, because creation is more alive in the truth of unity shared with one another.

Eros, the Greek god of love, reveals eroticism's expanse when we consider that in the Latin, this god is named Amor (Love) and Cupid (Desire). The Whiteheads, a pastoral theologian and developmental psychologist duo, describe eros as "the vital energy that courses through the world, animating every living thing . . . the force that quickens our hearts when we encounter suffering and moves us to help and heal." Eroticism's primary concern is interconnection, wholeness, healing—within oneself, with each other, and in the world around us. The meeting of the mystical and the erotic creates a force of wordless depth, a place of boundless connection and continual transcendence.

That's not to say that the way of the mystic is never lonely, because it often is. The mystic's ability to reach those moments of union emerges from a deep union with their own inner world. The mystic connects and nurtures their inner world so that they might connect with the Divine, the beloved, their community, and/or nature more deeply.

Eroticism is all too often misunderstood by those whose lives are led by patriarchy, Eurocentricity, whiteness, and heteronormativity—where LGBTQIA+ folks are often viewed through a lens of fear. Those who misunderstand eroticism regularly use heteronormativity as the ground from which to oversexualize LGBTQIA+ folks. Heteronormativity and patriarchy regularly minimize queer life to one's sexual encounters in (or outside of) the bedroom, suggesting that LGBTQIA+ lives are *only* sexual, in order to maintain a false narrative around power, control, and domination. By oversexualizing the LGBTQIA+ community (a tactic used on other marginalized groups as well), the dominant culture reduces queer folks to only one aspect of our lives. Similarly, bisexual, asexual, and pansexual folks (among others) often find their identities disbelieved (when in a heterosexual-presenting relationship, for instance), or diminished (when in a queer-presenting relationship) by the "normative" narrative. Additionally, relationship structures like polyamory are frequently overlooked by the dominant narrative of monogamy.

Queering mysticism means queering our inner stance. It means unifying body and spirit. By queering mysticism, we allow others and ourselves to unveil this rich truth of transcendence: that mysticism and the erotic are both part of our mutual flourishing.

EMBODIED MYSTICAL EXPRESSION

In 2021, I began a new podcast titled *Contemplating Now*, exploring the intersection of contemplation, mysticism, and social action. I learned from podcast guests that contemplation and mysticism exist in many expressions: embodied, erotic, unitive, interdependent, and solitary.

For each episode, I began by asking interviewees how they define both contemplation and mysticism. This question took shape for me when I first read the words of Rev. Dr. Barbara A. Holmes in her book *Joy Unspeakable: Contemplative Practices of the Black Church*. There, she writes about public mysticism, in which a mystic manifests public action for communal well-being. The public mystics she names include activists like Fannie Lou Hamer, Harriet Tubman, Rosa Parks, and Martin Luther King Jr. She writes that these public mystics are "seeking the ineffable in the ordinary, the mystical in the mundane, the transcendent in the midst of pragmatic justice-seeking acts." This scholarship invites us into considering the mystics outside of the expected norms, outside of what scholarship might point us to. Who are the activists in our midst seeking love, justice, and liberation for all people? Who are the musicians, poets, and artists expressing truths only found in transcending the here and now?

Holmes reflects on the ways mysticism and activism collide, bringing inward experience to the outward movement of communal well-being. The mystical, embodied encounter is as disruptive as it is unitive. Dr. Lerita Coleman Brown uses a similar term when she writes about sacred activists: those who are grounded in Spirit and "who invite Spirit's guidance about *how to take action, when to take action, what to say,* and *when to say it.*"

This is where "union and incarnation merge," writes Dr. Joy R. Bostic as she explores African American women's mystical encounters. She calls the mystical encounter a moment of such inward transformation that one is "compelled to respond to this encounter by way of embodied action."

Reading the work of Black women on mysticism, embodiment, and incarnational encounter, I discovered a way of examining mysticism that took hold of my imagination and contemplative life in dynamic ways. Yes, mysticism can be found in falling in love with a tree or in the eroticism in oceanic oneness with one's partner. But it is crucial to also recall that mysticism occurs in social-justice activism, and in being awake—and responsive to the injustices in one's community and the world. Mysticism happens in protest, when spirit meets body in the call for common good, liberation, and community thriving. Mysticism thrums through the world, calling for unity, and this requires our inner stance to be open to the truth of our interconnection.

Activism is mystical not only in the way it interrupts the status quo but also in the way it disrupts the continuation of harm. And when it comes to resisting the perpetuation of harm and violence, theologian Dr. Dorothee Sölle reminds us that mysticism's relationship to resistance is unequivocal: "Resistance is not the outcome of mysticism, resistance is mysticism itself."

Mysticism is queer—it cannot be harnessed, named, or claimed in any way—and that is one of the greatest wonders of the contemplative's path into mysticism. Definitions we bring to mysticism—and queerness—are usually futile attempts to limit what is named or to harness it with structures of dominance. Mysticism evaporates the boundaries of words as soon as they are spoken, because mysticism is about merging, cultivating depth of connection, and the erasure of false borders and boundaries between us. Mysticism is found in the ways we transcend expectation, forgo structures of harm, disrupt the status quo, and engage with the depth of our interconnection. And mystical union is truly a place where, in the words of Sölle, we have "borrowed the eyes of God." When we queer mysticism, we see that the pursuit of justice, love, liberation—and even joy and rest—stand within reach.

AN INVITATION TO QUEER MYSTICISM

Dr. Miguel H. Díaz (he/him/his)

This interview for the *Queering Contemplation* podcast took place October 25, 2022, on Zoom.

I came across the work of Dr. Díaz when his book *Queer God de Amor* was released. Boldly exploring St. John of the Cross (Juan de la Cruz) as a saint of the erotic and of queerness, Dr. Díaz goes to the heart of the matter in the life of this saint. In my conversation with Dr. Díaz, he shared that "God is the queerest of all realities." He suggests the ways that queer image, that queer reality, is upon each and every being—something both mystical and erotic:

There is something profoundly queer and mystical in the image of God, that all of us are born with. And it is that kind of a thirst to know more, of not being settled, of this dynamic, fluid, and ever open-ended reality that we have been created in the image of. By nature, we too are mystery, we too are an open-ended poem. Created in God's image, we are by nature dynamic creatures: fluid, intended to be open, to be recreated again and again and again as a result of human relationships and our relationships. And our relationship to God that is mediated in and through those relationships.

When I say something like "I read Juan [St. John of the Cross] as a very queer mystic," people might say, "What do you mean by these two terms: *queer* and *mystic*?" I then say, *Okay, consider what mystics do.* Consider what the mystics want us to do, which is to not settle into idolatry. The mystics want us to embrace our innate desire for the infinite, knowing there is an infinite God who defies all kinds of expectations and definitions.

Regardless of what his own sexual orientation, gender identity, was, this isn't the point here. I'm not saying Juan de la Cruz is queer in the sense of a very limited sexual or gender understanding. I say that Juan de la Cruz is queer in the sense that he embraced this disruptive practice that questions and does not settle for easy answers, binaries, black/white, documented/undocumented, male/female, straight/gay, etc. In that sense, and from that perspective, I think that mystics such as Juan de la Cruz are natural allies.

5 | BOUNDLESS LIMITS
Queering Ritual

> There are many queer possibilities and indeed many
> queer images already in our traditions. However, we
> have to look beyond the straight mind if we are to begin
> to grasp more of the divine nature; the parts that we
> have hidden away out of fear.
>
> —Lisa Isherwood, "Queering Christ:
> Outrageous Acts and Theological Rebellions"

Throughout life, we see and experience rituals related to death,
new life, marriage, religious sacraments, beginnings and endings,
and holiday celebrations. By definition, rituals are ceremonial,
related to religion, or associated with a social norm.

Queerness in ritual is mischief amid expectations. Queerness
is the expanse within ritual, keeping it alive beyond the ceremony,
beyond the sound, beyond the expectation, beyond what only our
senses can fathom. Queerness is the deepening of our routines
into rituals when we sense an internal bow to everything sacred.

The trickster figure, which appears in the literature and
myth of many Indigenous cultures, is a crafty mischief-maker
who flouts rules, makes others laugh, and demonstrates deep
wisdom. Author Dr. Miguel De La Torre says the trickster is one

who "constantly disrupts the established norm to reveal bad faith and hypocrisy, who shouts from the mountain top the secrets that exclude, who audaciously refuses to stay in an assigned space."

Queerness is the trickster that helps us to circumvent the harmful aspects of *same-old* rituals, *same-old* ways of being, *same-old* expectations. In this way, queerness enlivens the possibility of equity and liberates ritual from supporting the dominative structures that limit us all. "A closed system is a trap," writes Anglican anchorite Maggie Ross, "and salvation is opening and liberating from traps. There is no salvation in a closed system." Queerness invites us into the salvific and liberating aspects of ritual itself. Queering ritual awakens the wild trickster in each of us.

But some rituals are rooted in oppressive systems, controlled by traditions, religions, gender constructs, Eurocentricity, whiteness, ableism, heteronormativity, or other constructs of dominance. Religious rituals, in particular, have at times been violent, harmful, and entirely unjust. Over the years religious rituals have been used to justify violent behavior, words, and actions. These rituals are often co-opted by the dominant group to perpetuate injustice, pain, and suffering.

But what, exactly, makes ritual innately queer? Or how can we queer ritual when we find it vacant of liberation, of love, of the wildness within? My experience of queering ritual includes examining the spaciousness of choice and imagination within the ritual itself. Ritual often invites us into spheres that can free us from the ordinary. Amid the bells at the monastery calling me at the time of prayer, I am centered in the possibility of the moment. Hearing the rhythmic creeds at an Episcopal church, I find my mind bursting with questions and doubts. Watching a friend get married, I am enlivened to the wildness of love in my own being.

When I contemplate the spiritual rituals in which I've participated, I see the ways they are undergirded by some kind of
mystery hosting the moment at hand. The origins of the word
spiritual relate, of course, to "spirit"; what might be less obvious
is that they are also concerned with breath, breathing, wind,
and air—*ruach* in the wording of the Hebrew Scriptures. The
etymology of *spiritual* dates back to the twelfth century, from the
medieval ecclesiastical use of Latin *spiritualis*. *Ritual* comes from
the sixteenth century, related to rites or religious rites and the
Latin *ritualis*.

But still, when I glance at the word *spiritual* queerly, with
my head tilted, I notice that it actually contains the word *ritual*.
While the last thing I claim is etymological expertise, what if
ritual was also an invitation into this breath, breathing, wind, or
air? Ethnographer Arnold van Gennep, who explored ritual as
it relates to the term he coined, *rites of passage*, wrote that all rites
of passage contain three key moments: separation, liminality,
and incorporation. What if rituals were meant to be expansive
moments of separation, or letting go; liminality, or being in the
unknown; and incorporation into our perpetual becoming, all
enmeshed with the expansiveness of breath? What if our rituals
could become breaths of fresh air—flowing, moving, expansive,
and ever-changing? What if ritual only reaches its boundless
limits when we queer it?

QUEERING CHAPLAINCY

While preparing for ordination, I was required to serve as a
hospital chaplain in training. It was a Catholic hospital, so for
most chaplains, numerous rituals went along with the job, but

as a woman, I was not "allowed" to perform many of them. I was assigned to a cohort with five others: a combination of men seeking ordination, a colleague who "didn't agree" with my "lifestyle" but "loved" me, and another Protestant who seemed stuck in the middle.

It was clear I was the token queer in this little group. My very presence queered the experience for us all. I resolved from the beginning, however, to focus on the humans I would get to accompany in their hospital rooms, rather than on the large disconnect in beliefs between my colleagues and me. Theological discourse across such a wide gap tends to rely on apologetics assuming the need to defend the existence of LGBTQIA+ folks, and I no longer waste any time on that. The innate belonging of LGBTQIA+ folks and our right to existence—to live, love, thrive, and be ourselves—is, for me, the only place where the conversation can begin.

Most days I was assigned to one of the floors where I met people who had experienced everything from gunshot wounds to terrible accidents. I had encounters with people struggling with memory issues, some who saw trees or children in the room when there were none, and those suffering from such immense trauma that they couldn't speak. Most often I simply sat and offered company. My biggest goal in this work was to extend the medical oath from my previous work in the counseling field: to do no harm, especially amid someone's already painful and vulnerable situation. I wanted to cultivate a space of love, safety, curiosity, support, and comfort.

But the chaplain's role signals religion, and sometimes that, in itself, can be stressful for patients who have previously encountered religious harm, abuse, or trauma. So each step into the hospital room began for me with the premise that I was there to visit only if they'd like, to check in and chat only if they wanted to. Queering my interactions, I'd often go off script. If the conversation led to prayer, we might pray. If the conversation led to cussing, we'd definitely cuss. If the conversation led to anxieties and worries, we'd sit together and mull over our questions. I queered the typical rituals and routines of the chaplain's role in these moments in order to care more deeply, see more expansively, cultivate connection, and do no harm.

Some days I worked with people who were experiencing the agony of stillbirth, next door to others holding the wonder of brand-new life. On one occasion, I was invited to a family's bedside for a naming ceremony for their stillborn infant, a ceremony that honors the child and the parents. Approaching the room, I assumed I would be speaking with the parents about their *plans* for a naming ceremony a bit later in the day. I imagined offering them support, talking with them to learn about their beliefs and feelings, planning for the ritual ahead. But as we began talking, I saw, out of the corner of my eye, that the child was with us in that precise moment. The baby, just the size of my palm, lay in a tiny basket with an even tinier blanket. I realized the ceremony was to take place immediately, during this visit.

So, with trembling voice, I began. Together we dove into a beautiful, heart-rending ceremony to honor the hope and awe of birth, the naming of their child, and the grief over such unfathomable loss. This small period in time—this ritual—became a temporary container for their boundless sorrow. Perhaps it was as much a way to name the grief in the room as to name the child.

NAMING WHAT IS QUEER

Some rituals we enact. Others are enacted *upon* us.

Names were important in my work as a chaplain. I always took a second glance at the list of patients before stepping into a room to ensure I was naming someone properly. Anthropologists Dr. Barbara Bodenhorn and Dr. Gabriele Vom Bruck write that naming is a "crucial aspect of converting 'anybodies' into 'somebodies.'" The act of calling someone by their name of choice cultivates respect, a sense of seeing and being seen. In my chaplaincy work, it also meant ensuring that the name on the patient list was correct and checking to see if the patient preferred to be called by a different chosen name or a nickname. Some didn't even know they had a choice in such a setting, while others corrected me immediately.

I didn't know where my own name, Cassidy, came from until I was in my thirties. To my surprise, there wasn't some fancy reasoning, like "My parents delighted in the Irish meaning," or "I have an ancestor by the same name." No, it was that my parents' "sex day" was Saturday, when they'd also watch a TV show called *Hopalong Cassidy*. Exactly. I was named after a male cowboy persona my parents watched on their "sex days." Honestly, in some weird way, I welcomed the information. Though I'd played around with shortening my name to "Cass" or "Cassie" (which never quite fit), I've never disliked my name, which certainly isn't the case for everyone.

In psychological discourse, naming is considered a symbolic behavior. There are naming ceremonies, practices, and rituals around the globe, some as simple as filling out the birth certificate. Religiously or spiritually, naming is often considered one of our first acts of freedom and self-expression, which humans have been doing since the creation stories in Genesis (naming the animals). Apart from the ways in which names are chosen, "proper names are never simply there, as nouns are, but must be bestowed in rituals of naming." In this way, naming claims a stake on our lives, often before we are even born. Others may go unnamed in utero and even days, weeks, or months after birth. Whenever our name arrives, it can be an act of hope, defiance, remembrance, chance, or proclamation—or it can imply limits or set bounds to our lives. Our names are usually chosen on our behalf, before we have a say in the matter. Some people are given names tied to an ancestor, bearing expectations, or to a title, insinuating personality. It can be fun if, say, a child named Happy, as my sister was nearly named, grows up to be a lady rapper who wears gold spandex suits—which my sister does! But that name also has the potential to feel like a heavy burden.

Ritual, naming, and queerness may not seem immediately connected. In fact, they may seem almost antithetical to one another. Ritual connotes clarity and consistency; as Dr. Felicitas Goodman notes, in ritual "each participant has a well-rehearsed role to act out. It takes place within a set time span and in a limited space, and involves a predetermined set of events." Similarly, names represent what we are addressing or referring to in a given moment. Meanwhile, queerness refuses to be a container and resists being told what to do.

How can we queer that which is already set, predetermined, or scripted? This is exactly what queerness does: disrupts the stagnant, shakes up the predetermined, rewrites the script—opening us up to more. Trans folks model what it means to queer names and pronouns more than any other group of people. They teach us not only what it means to continually become who we are, but also the importance and beauty of naming and sometimes renaming—or expressing our ongoing becoming in more formal ways.

According to *Collins Dictionary*, the study of names, known as onomatology, comes from a Greek word meaning "collector of words." And I find that as we grow, we collect and shed names and descriptions of ourselves. Names we are given as infants, names from our lovers, nicknames from friends, alter egos we give ourselves, names and/or words of description: these are all a part of our ever-evolving, breathing existence.

Many people are finding a way to queer the act of naming. When we use nicknames, we play with names through a lens of personality or by looking at the name differently, sideways, upside-down, or in shortened form. While we are all provided with the symbolic and sometimes ritualistic container of being named—or when someone decides our gender at birth based on sex organs—it isn't until we queer or embrace our name and our pronouns that they become our own. It is only when the ritual is queered for ourselves, in a way of our choosing, that something becomes *ours*. Something feels *more* like us, and something is distilled into clarity—often, perhaps, just the clarity of continual wondering, exploration, and unfolding.

For others, queering or asserting one's name and pronouns has meant a legal name change to reflect a gender, agender, or non-binary identity consistent with themselves. Neopronouns, for instance, come into play by utilizing a word "to serve as a pronoun without expressing gender, like 'ze' and 'zir.' . . . Neopronouns give people who feel different from the rest of the world a way to avoid all its boxes at once." And for others, queering a name or sharing one's pronouns has meant engaging their understanding of self with their given name or gender identity. Queering and expressing our names and identities awaken us to something beyond limits and expectations. This awakening can give us breathing room to not contort ourselves into others' assumptions.

"My chosen name and pronouns—they/them—don't tell the world exactly who I am," Rev. M. Jade Kaiser, the cofounder of enfleshed, shared with me. "But they do close some of the gap between who I am and how strangers or beloveds understand me. For me, the name and pronouns assigned to me at birth were misleading—setting up an immediate and unnecessary barrier to relationship. Exchanging that language for words that more closely align with my sense of self enables not only my own flourishing but also offers a more authentic starting place for relationships with others."

TRANSFORMATIVE RITUALS

Sometimes I am queering the ritual, and other times the ritual is queering me.

Both queerness and ritual require an engaged imagination, open to possibility outside of limitations. Both queerness and ritual can guide us through binaries of gender and sexuality, of all that is known and unknown. Ritual without queerness becomes rote, stripped of its transformative power. Ritual without queerness is minimized to a stagnant condition, unable to grow or move beyond what isn't working.

Routines and rituals can also meld together. The morning cup of coffee becomes a sacred process of movement and pauses, senses and stillness. The evening walk shifts into a meditative trance of watching the ducks in the nearby pond. My routines become rituals the second I sense an internal bow to the moment's entanglement with holiness, with mindfulness, with love, wonder and awe. In ritual, I am rooted and invited to dive deeper into the expanse of myself and my own unfolding. The mindful shift of acknowledgment takes me into more spaciousness, questions, and curiosities. Without my routines and rituals—and my routines *shifting* into rituals from time to time—I don't think I'd be as alive and awake to my own personhood. I wouldn't know my true self as clearly or as deeply.

But I've often pushed up against religious rituals—not because I have some disdain for authority (though I absolutely do), but because religious rituals often dictate a theology or an action. In many religious rituals, I am not just told *what* to do but also *how* to perform a ceremonial act. For example, religious leaders might tell us to close our eyes for prayer. But I keep my eyes open during times of prayer, be it a public prayer or a gathering for silent prayer. Things are internally noisier for me when my eyes are closed. When my eyes are open, if I can soften my gaze upon an object—a candle flame, the wood grain in the floor, or a liturgical item of some sort—I am much more prone to settle.

Ritual also frequently offers me some inexplicable sense of freedom. While traveling to Trappist monasteries, I often felt a strange sensation of freedom. Hearing the bells calling the community to prayer seven times a day felt like a homecoming. The hours of work combined with prayer gave me a sense of rhythm that soothed me. The irony—of rituals feeling like a loving freedom—is not lost on me. When ritual comes as an invitation, a choice to engage or not engage, limits are expanded because freedom is present. And from this place, where ritual meets freedom, our relationship to self, others, and the Divine can be continually deepened.

I once mentioned my curiosity about this seeming contradiction to a monk at Mepkin Abbey in South Carolina. He resonated with my attempt to make sense of this strangeness: that choosing rituals can feel like choosing freedom. Having lived in this tension as a monk for over twenty years, he responded with his own question: "Culturally, any boundary that is seen as a limitation is perceived as *bad*. But when you choose these self-limits, do they open you to a reality that is only accessible because you've chosen those limitations?"

Reflecting on this, I wonder: Does the air come in, does the flow expand, and does the weirdness and strangeness of ritual find its innate queerness *only* once we begin to engage in the ritual itself (whether it is one of our own making or another)? Is the choice to engage or partake in the spiritual practice the precise thing that opens me up to more?

The monk's comment stays with me. In the moments I've found myself questioning my own religion—the choice to even be a Christian—I've recognized there's an aspect of ritual's boundless limits related to my choice. When atheist friends or friends of different faiths ask me why I stick with Christianity when it has caused so much harm and pain in the world, I usually respond—queerly—with a Buddhist saying: "If you want to strike water, you don't dig six 1-foot wells; you dig one 6-foot well."

Christianity is the tradition I was birthed into, the well in which I continue to dig without limits. Christian faith is the well I am rooted in through my ancestors, the one in which I have the possibility of going deep in the name of healing, justice, liberation, and love. The water of the Divine can be drawn from other traditions of faith, or no traditions of faith. But this particular well is the one I have chosen. Christianity is the set of religious rituals I choose to engage with—the spirituality I experience as innately queer and find ways to queer—in order to reclaim its possibility for healing, justice, liberation, and love.

AN INVITATION TO QUEER RITUAL

Rev. Mihee Kim-Kort (she/her/hers)

This interview for the *Queering Contemplation* podcast took place December 12, 2022, on Zoom.

I came across Rev. Mihee's work when she was invited to speak at the Christian Theological Seminary in Indianapolis where I was studying. I picked up her book *Outside the Lines: How Embracing Queerness Will Transform Your Faith*, and I was awakened by her voice, which affirms the reader on every page with statements like "Queerness begins from the premise that bodies matter." I had a chance to chat with Rev. Mihee on the *Queering Contemplation* podcast, where we discussed the magic of queerness and the many ways it gives us a new way into something. In the conversation, she shared with me how she has queered ritual in her work as a pastor and a lifelong learner:

> What does it really mean to say that queerness is magic? For me, I think that there is something about the divine, the otherworldly. And not just something sort of ineffable, but something that is very imminent, and human, flesh and blood, but that it also suggests its own sort of category. It's

not science, and it's not totally religion; it's not something that fits some of the logics and grammars that we use for other things. And I love that, because [in] some of the more indigenous and shamanistic cultures, which my family come from, I read and hear of the rituals, spirit possession, and the way magic is sort of intertwined in a lot of the indigenous sort of cultures in Korea. We're not talking doctrine or theology here—it feels more real, in a lot of ways.

In my doctoral program, you have to take two foreign languages, and one of them I decided would be Korean, because I'd grown up speaking it a little bit. I bring that up because I like the possibility of asking: How do we shape our reality with the kind of language that we use? And so sometimes, the word *queer* feels hard-edged to me [as] in if we're just saying a person is queer, or you use that as a mark of identity. But there's something about queerness and queering which—to go back to the way that I understand queerness and being queer—is playful, to play with the language a little bit. And in playing with the language, it gives us another opportunity and another possibility of how it can be useful.

Queering gives me another way into things like spirituality—understanding things like prayer, and worship, and liturgy. So it's not only one way of doing prayer and one way of liturgy, or one way of doing any kind of worship or anything that's sort of associated with faith and spirituality. That's another thing about queerness: that it might have a lot of different kinds of names. It's just one of those things that you can't really capture—it's always going to be in excess of the sort of lines that you try to put around it.

6 | BOTTOMLESS CREATIVITY
Queering Boredom

> Might we consider boredom as not only necessary for our life but also as one of its greatest blessings? A gift, pure and simple, a precious chance to be alone with our thoughts and alone with God?
>
> —Kathleen Norris, *Acedia & Me:*
> *A Marriage, Monks, and a Writer's Life*

"I want to be bored with you," my partner writes to me on our very first silent Saturday together.

That's the shortest love letter I've ever received, I think to myself and smile.

We sit silently, side by side, passing back and forth a sketch-book, slowly adding trees, birds, stars, water, and moonlight. She fills my lake with the cosmos, and I gather grass around the base of her tree. Soon we get bored with this, look at each other with softness, and laugh. The sun has set, and the biggest show on earth—the birdwatching—has subsided for the day. So all we have is what's here. The rootedness of the connection we are continuing to deepen is beyond words. Our eye contact is more knowing, our smiles filled with affection, and our touch more tender.

But as much as I love boredom, I also fear it. Subconsciously I equate boredom with emptiness, nothingness, limited time, death. Boredom reminds me of the void. I often fear that if I'm bored, I am not doing *enough*, I am not being *enough*, I am not *enough*.

This fear runs throughout our culture. We live in a society that moves on the hinges of productivity and capitalism, demanding more from us all. In many ways, if we are no longer doing or making, the world tells us, we're no longer here, we no longer exist. In reality, non-productivity, emptiness, boredom, and even the act of relinquishing control—these are often the nutrients of the most meaningful things humans have ever done or made, including love, delight, pleasure, and rest.

But boredom isn't something we can construct or conjure through desire—we cannot muster up boredom out of thin air. Dr. Helen E. Lees, author of *Silence in Schools*, said in an interview for the documentary film *In Pursuit of Silence* that she, like many people, sometimes tries to slow her pace: "And if that becomes boring, good. Because there's a lot of value in 'boring.' Why should we always be stimulated, or more and more stimulated, so we reach a fever pitch, and what happens, where do you go next?"

The only way to engage boredom is to meet it on its own terms, for what it offers, because *it is*. The *is-ness* of boredom is the simplicity of meeting the present moment—the moment I frequently fail to engage with. And the *is-ness* of boredom holds a kind of ambiguity, which is exactly what makes it queer. Boredom is an odd state of being to engage with and to delight in. But queering boredom is about redeeming its *is-ness*: when we queer boredom, we're returned to the present moment, overflowing with possibility and gratitude.

Contemplation and contemplative life are not synonymous with boredom, but the contemplative does have a special relationship with boredom. Boredom is filled with fecundity and profound discernment, a place of centering and guidance, a place of expanse, a place also queer by its nature—moving in all directions, no direction, and holding no expectations.

THE HAUNT OF DEATH IN BOREDOM

Boredom is a queer invitation into the present moment. Boredom is a reminder to let go of the need to *do* or *be* beyond what already *is*. And although boredom often haunts us with reminders of death's seemingly final say, it also reminds us to surrender to life's natural cycles. In fact, the phrase *memento mori*, Latin for "remember that you will die," has been a part of the philosophical tradition since ancient Rome. *Memento mori* was used as a means to awaken humans to the present moment, knowing that one day we will no longer be here. In the Christian tradition, we might relate this to the annual Lenten reference to Genesis 3:19, where the Hebrew Scriptures remind us, "You are dust, and to dust you shall return." Alongside this reminder, the use of *memento mori* as a kind of meditative practice has long existed in Catholicism through the work of saints, modern-day monastics, and authors who have even suggested we keep a small skull on our desk to remember we will die.

Alongside this remembering, I think of the monasteries all over the US that are dying because of a lack of novitiates (incoming monks, nuns, monastics). Aging populations of monks, with few or no new novices, find themselves having to navigate what is next for their land and legacy. In the meantime, they're inadvertently teaching the rest of us something about how to accept death. It's not only dying well that they're teaching us; they are also teaching us how to surrender to all we cannot control. Is it possible our daily dance with boredom is one of the many things we are invited to surrender to?

Over ten years ago, on my travels to monasteries, I found myself in the small town of Ava, Missouri, tucked in the foothills of the Ozarks. At the time, Assumption Abbey was undergoing a new and dramatic change. The monks were aging and dying with no new monks coming in. While deciding what to do about this problem—whether to close or shift course—the monks of Missouri met with a Cistercian community from Vietnam. Together they decided to launch a program that brought mutual benefit. Some Vietnamese Cistercian monks would come and join the community of Assumption Abbey and live side by side with the monks. If this exchange was deemed a success after some years, Assumption Abbey would be formally transferred to the Vietnamese congregation of the Cistercian Order.

Across the country, other monastic communities are changing as well. The monks at Holy Trinity Abbey in Huntsville, Utah, were aging, and with no incoming monks, the monastery had to close its doors in 2017. But before the aging monastics moved to a nearby senior living center, they organized an agreement to sell the land to local conservationists seeking easements to protect the land, including the cemetery where the remaining monks would join upon their deaths.

These surrenders, these deaths—as ends and new beginnings, creating a fecundity of legacy absent of ego—astonish me. These actions are not only free of ego and productivity; they honor the reality of life's interconnection and cycles of death and life. They honor what *is*.

Since I went on those travels, only fifteen of the seventeen Trappist monasteries in the US remain, with whispers from others about their possible closure. What *new* life, I wonder, will their deaths bring? What growth, harvest, or new cycles will arise on the land, and what echoes of prayer will impact those who come after them? What depth of possibilities exist within these deaths? Will any of these dying monasteries work with local Indigenous leaders to participate in returning the land to those who originally occupied it?

Witnessing how these monasteries have closed, and the legacy they leave behind, eases my anxiety about boredom, death, and even surrender. But the clock keeps ticking as a haunting reminder of limited time for *doing* and *being* on earth. Despite knowing that these monks did all they could to recruit new novices so the monastery could continue, I still wonder how they hold all that's been left behind. The land remains. And their lifetimes of prayers—seven times a day—are still with me, ingrained in my memory and a part of the earth's atmosphere. With their bodies below the earth on the land they committed to, the very lives and deaths of these contemplatives teach me the path of letting go, releasing control, and surrendering to the depth of possibility in the present moment.

What would happen if surrendered to boredom, honoring it as a place lush with wonder, a space of fecundity, and a starting point for respecting the present moment? What would happen if we queered the way we looked at boredom, seeing how the haunt of death can draw us closer to what *is*?

The contemplative response to these stories, we might assume, is to bask in the beauty of the present moment, to no longer fear death, to give ourselves to the magic of boredom and life's cycles—but that just isn't true for us all. The truth is that these stories remind us to have a healthier relationship with the *is-ness* of each day, including the pondering of death amid our experiences of boredom. These stories invite us to carry our own ideas of legacy lightly so that we might more deeply engage in the present moment, so that we might see the potential for depth beyond our mind's bounds.

APATHETIC BOREDOM

During my monastic travels, someone suggested I read Kathleen Norris's *Acedia & Me: A Marriage, Monks, and a Writer's Life*. The title baffled me, and at the time I wondered what the hell it had to do with me. It turns out I had yet to realize just how meaningful the book would become.

Acedia is a kind of spiritual apathy, and from its Greek root it suggests an absence of care. Acedia is what happens to us when we're thrashing around in boredom alongside a sense of hopelessness. Used in monastic and medieval literature, forms of the word *acedia* have mysteriously woven themselves in and out of the lexicon since the fourteenth century. Norris points out, however, that acedia was first named and explored by the fourth-century Christian monk Evagrius Ponticus and the fourth-century desert monastic Amma Theodora.

As I listened to the audio version of Norris's book on my walks around various monasteries, I began to better understand my own experiences with boredom and its relationship with time, death, and even depression. Norris's work gave me an understanding of the spiritual dimensions of isolation and why those experiences vary in different times, contexts, and situations.

It's important to understand the ways spiritual apathy can find us in times of boredom. Those times of stirring in boredom, Norris tells us, may in fact be forms of acedia. The "restless boredom, frantic escapism, commitment phobia, and enervating despair that plague us today is the ancient demon of acedia in modern dress," Norris writes. And in a more expansive definition, she states, "Acedia is not a relic of the fourth century or a hang-up of some weird Christian monks, but a force we ignore at our peril. . . . Wherever we run to escape it, acedia is there, propelling us to 'the next best thing.' . . . Acedia has come so far with us that it easily attaches to our hectic and overburdened schedules. We appear to be anything but slothful, yet that is exactly what we are, as we do more and care less, and feel pressured to do still more." Boredom finds itself in—or perhaps even morphs into—acedia when we are busier than ever but remain tethered to a sense of emptiness.

Queerness has the potential to redeem boredom's *is-ness* by helping us recognize its fullness without having to *do* anything. Is it possible we could avoid things like acedia by beginning to queer the ways we embrace boredom? Boredom can be a very bountiful place, a place the contemplative revels in, and a place queerly filled with imagination, rest, and a deepening of one's roots—in place, relationship, and community.

Distinguishing between these two—boredom and acedia— is a task of discernment and a call to queerness. I find myself asking very specific questions of myself in boredom, in solitude, and in therapy that help bring that discernment to bear:

Am I wanting to be in "hermit mode" because I need to think clearly—or because I am avoiding?

Do I want to say "no" to everything to instill good boundaries—or because I'm withdrawing?

Do I not want to be around others because I'm truly exhausted—or because I'm shrinking from connection?

What fear might be blocking me from queering boredom into *is-ness*, connection, rest, or fecundity?

Finally, it's crucial to remember that acedia should not be confused with clinical depression. When things like boredom, spiritual apathy, and listlessness form a place of depression—when we can no longer shift to boredom's *is-ness* in the present moment—we may need to reach out to a therapist, our partner, a friend, a family member, or even a hotline. We may need help from one of these supports to keep ourselves out of danger.

BEING BORED TO BE BORED

Boredom during childhood was one of our greatest tools for imagination. When my siblings and I got bored during long car drives, we'd make up car games that resulted in new ways of looking at the landscape rushing past us. Making up stories about the cars driving by, we'd engage our imagination's potential for endless creativity. Years later, I got my first cell phone, with its invitation to distraction and avoidance. A few years later, a TV appeared in nearly every room of our house and computers in several rooms.

Each decade of my life has held its own set of tools for "curing" boredom instead of recognizing that boredom was the tool for our imagination. Along with each piece of technology came the increasing potential for avoiding the interior questions and explorations boredom asks. In earlier years I engaged my imagination to decide how to not be bored, or even embraced the moment by just staring out the window. Now I sometimes find myself mindlessly scrolling, often ignoring imagination all together. At times I even resist boredom's abundancy in rest by doing more and more throughout the day, tricking myself into thinking there's no time to be still.

I need to reply to that work email.
I should check in with my friend.
I really need to work on that house project.
I should really edit that writing.
I ought to go move my body.

The decision I make in any particular moment—whether to *be* in the boredom or to *do* in the boredom—happens in a second or less. More frequently I choose the *doing.* But every time I truly slow down and make the opposite decision—to just *be*—I inevitably sink into the fruits of the present moment, the *is-ness* of what's here.

I live across the street from a park where my favorite squirrels and birds reside. Almost daily I go on a morning walk. I mindfully go around and around in the same way and on the same path until I am done. Like a meditation or mindfulness practice, the walk and its repetition soothe me and frequently fill me with ideas and creativity. The walk's routine—its very boredom— reveals to me a blank slate for the day. And my walks confirm what many studies reveal about boredom: it stimulates creativity and its frequent companion, problem-solving.

When I am truly walking to walk—and not just for health purposes, or to listen to the next podcast episode, or to make calls—walking feels like a pretty simple event. When I walk for a purpose or to be productive, I not only fail the present moment; I often miss out on the *is-ness* of the walk itself. But walking simply for walking's sake simplifies and distills the present moment into the truth of what it *is*. When my mind is centered in focused attention, the rest of myself is freed up to *be*, often to the point that I forget the singular act or way of being as it is happening.

I think of my late friend Jim Forest, a peace activist who held a deep friendship with Thich Nhat Hanh, the Vietnamese Buddhist monk who made a tremendous mark on the world. Thich Nhat Hanh crafted a lesson in the mindfulness found in boredom through a story he shared:

> One night, Jim asked if he might do the dishes. I said, "Go ahead, but if you wash the dishes you must know the way to wash them." Jim replied, "Come on, you think I don't know how to wash the dishes?" I answered, "There are two ways to wash the dishes. The first is to wash the dishes in order to have clean dishes and the second is to wash the dishes in order to wash the dishes." Jim was delighted and said, "I choose the second way—to wash the dishes to wash the dishes." From then on, Jim knew how to wash the dishes. I transferred the "responsibility" to him for an entire week.

Though different, boredom and mindfulness are similar in how they bring us to the present moment. Mindfulness is an ever-present companion in the contemplative's life. Unlike a mindfulness or contemplative practice, boredom usually doesn't pop up as a thing we choose. But what if boredom was a practice we *could* choose when it presents itself?

Without knowing it, sometimes we do choose boredom. Sometimes we really walk to walk, we are bored to be bored, or we are still to be still. Sometimes we choose the route of *is-ness,* the way of *being,* the path of boredom.

QUEER COMMITMENT TO BOREDOM

Early one morning, I stepped out on the porch and held up my hand to my ear to signal to my partner that I could hear the swans' wings taking flight off the lake nearby. She looked at me knowingly and smiled. Sometimes when we're sharing coffee in the morning, we ask each other for silence as a way to co-regulate and rest our nervous systems as we ease into the day. But this shared silence is also an invitation into the boredom, the present moment, the depth and deepening between us, and newness as birthed from the death of sleep from which we have emerged.

Queering boredom is an invitation into *being* rather than another invitation to *do.* Boredom awakens us to the reality contemplative life is founded upon—it reminds us that everything is here, now. Each time we choose boredom, we sink more deeply into the seat of reality.

Queering boredom reminds us to reclaim, redeem, and remain where we find ourselves. This kind of showing up to the moment is a commitment to the present in time, place, and relationship. Inevitably, the longer we remain in these moments, the more we get to see: of place, of people, the Divine, and ourselves. This, of course, isn't always lovely, because sometimes you show up like a frigid, windy winter day amid your partner's summer. Or they show up like a rainy spring amid your autumn. But without seeing this in our relationships, and without letting ourselves be seen *in* this, our relationships can become shallow. If we can only be present to our loved one's good moods, or summer days, we fail at loving the fullness of who they are and how we can nurture each other's winters. Just as boredom invites us into the present moment, it also invites us into the truth of what that moment holds.

In this way, queer boredom—committed to the present moment—is a willingness to understand and grow through the season we find ourselves, and each other, in. This commitment to remaining reminds us of the seasons within and around us— that our winters will turn to springs, that our summers will bring the colors of autumn. Choosing boredom at times resembles choosing to stay in the more difficult moments, in the uncomfortable place, to stick with ourselves and our loved one in the *is-ness* of what's here (unless that is harmful to our or their wellbeing). And queering how we look at boredom allows us to see the present moment's possibility of deepening connection.

A couple of weeks after I raised my hand to my ear as the swans took flight, my partner and I were inside by a window, again cradling our morning cups of coffee in shared silence. Having accepted the moment's invitation, we quietly checked in with ourselves while sitting close enough to feel one another's warmth. Suddenly, I felt her gaze turn to me, and she looked at me like she had just had the most incredible revelation. Her eyes widened with wonder and childlike awe. She stood up and announced, as if she were reciting a Mary Oliver poem, "Sandhill cranes! Hurry outside!" With admiration and awe, I followed her beckoning.

Sure enough, there they were: a flock of sandhill cranes cruising in the skies above on their seasonal trip somewhere warmer, somewhere together, somewhere in the *is-ness* of now.

As my partner and I watched them, side by side, I was reminded of boredom's fecundity—that the cycles of growth, life, and even emotions are ever before me, like birds in flight. I was reminded that in boredom, everything is possible and nothing needs to happen. I was reminded, *In this moment, here and now, next to her, is the moment where it all is, where life resides.* I was reminded by my partner that when we listen deeply, look wholly, and surrender our senses to the present moment, we get to embrace its *is-ness*; we get to witness the sandhill cranes in flight.

INVITATION TO QUEER BOREDOM

Assata de la Cruz (she/her/hers)

This interview for the *Queering Contemplation* podcast took place on July 14, 2023, at the Wild Goose Festival and July 21, 2023, via email.

While at the Wild Goose Festival in 2023, I sat down with Assata de la Cruz, a Queer Black Indigenous medicine woman. She's the executive director of the traditional wellness community Savage Daughters and the director of community outreach for Soulforce, an organization for Queer folks reclaiming our spirits from weaponized religion. When we sat down to chat, we began by exploring the ways Assata views and experiences "Queer" in her own life, and the ways she has experienced boredom as a form of resistance:

I don't need to define anything. I don't need to check off boxes. I don't need a reason that makes sense for the greater majority. This is the beauty of Queerness. I can do absolutely nothing for the sake of doing absolutely nothing. I can do it just because I want to. "I want to" is a full sentence, a full response. Connecting to my Queerness empowered me to stand firm in my boredom.

The idea of being constant producers was ingrained in Black and Indigenous people specifically, by the infiltration of white Christian supremacy into our culture as a means to end our existence. So much of reclaiming my traditional roots is reclaiming my boredom that was stolen from us.

I believed in the "strong Black woman" trope that I was force-fed by a society that I now recognize was committed to my destruction. But I played along. I watched my mother play along, and her mother. Then the more I watched *her* mother (my great-grandmother), I realized she lived her life differently. She was always . . . just bored. I couldn't wrap my head around it and it was many years before I would even begin to understand the resilience of the way she lived. But I very distinctly remember that being the first time I had a glimpse of another world being popular.

It wouldn't be until almost a decade later when my body forced me to start reimagining another way of life. I spent the majority of early adulthood in and out of hospitals because I ignored my body's whispers to "slow the heck down." So much of my worth was tied to how much I could contribute. I was convinced I would simply outwork a system that I don't think I fully understood as a system at the time. Fast-forward to me being thirty years old. Toward the end of my first pregnancy, my body's whispers turned into screams, which would eventually lead to a diagnosis of Lupus SLE. I was physically incapable of "pulling myself up by the bootstraps" I'd worked so hard to be able to afford in the first place. Learning more about my disease and how much it is exacerbated by stress caused me to have to reevaluate my entire identity at this point, which was completely defined by being a "girl boss." Learning that Lupus SLE is predominantly seen in Black women is what really catapulted my revolt against capitalist culture and started me viewing my boredom as the ultimate resistance. Queering boredom is saying no. Queering boredom is refusing to see the world in binaries: producer vs. lazy. It's much more nuanced than this.

7 | UNLIMITED BECOMING
Queering the True Self

It's a privilege to live in a time when we're permitted to wonder. We have this gift because of our queer ancestors—trans and nonbinary and genderqueer people who did the analysis and taught the history lessons, who put their own bodies in harm's way . . . so that we could have space to wonder out loud. It's a gift to hold this sacred trust. We hold it with fear and trembling, because it's so sacred. We also hold it lightly and with delight, because it's so sacred. We are permitted to play. We are permitted to be this free.

—Laura Jean Truman

"When did you know?"

"How did you find out you were queer?"

"When did you first realize you liked women?"

"You're lucky; it'd be so much easier if I liked women."

"I wish I were queer."

Like many queer folks, I have heard these questions and comments often. The questions come from different angles, few of which are surprising to me. And I'm not always the recipient; sometimes I am the one who is curious about another's experience.

Why?

We usually ask questions like this—and sometimes over-ask them—because we're seeking our own comfort or self-understanding. Our questions might come from pondering the vastness of the Divine's image upon, within, or all around us. But I'm all too familiar with the harm of certitude, assumptions, and internalized dispositions toward norms and expectations.

Even if we let go of the need to know or understand, our society still obsesses about naming, claiming, and defining. As I worked on my documentary film about Thomas Merton, I listened to audio clips of his stream-of-consciousness thoughts from his hermitage, and I especially resonated with this line: "I know in my heart that I do not need to be defined, I do not need to define myself, and yet I have this allergy of definition."

Like most of us, I've spent a large chunk of my life figuring out, naming, and identifying the things around me. As an ennea-gram 5, I have an insatiable appetite to know, understand, and learn, and I can get stuck in the desire to name, define, or identify. But when we reach to trap anything in a definition, we also trap ourselves. A desire to define or know does not give me permission to ask questions simply to satisfy my own curiosity. Rather, the desire to name, define, or identify is a different invitation alto-gether. It's an invitation for me to examine and hold openhanded my *own* definition, my *own* name, and my *own* identity, over and over again.

And while no one owes anyone else answers to such ques-tions, *ever*, I believe we can subvert institutions like patriarchy and heteronormativity by recognizing that we ourselves never fully know the answers. We are ever evolving, ever becoming, and ever unfolding. Identity is an ever-moving target, and any conviction that the self is singular or fixed is limiting and often even harmful. Instead, we can hold what we think we know about ourselves with open hands. We can allow ourselves to *become*, which offers us room to breathe and blossom. Maybe when sexuality and gender forgo binary expectations, they are freer to be alive within us. And contemplative life beckons us to the same: encouraging us to loosen our grip on ourselves, those around us, and the Divine.

So, when did I first know I was queer?

When did I realize I was attracted to women?

When did I think heterosexuality was not the societal script I was to follow?

Looking back through my childhood photos, I see a picture of me from a sleepover with two other girls. We're probably about seven years old, and my friends are both wearing shiny, silky nightgowns. I stand next to them in an oversized Minnesota Vikings T-shirt. Another photo shows me with my bowl-cut hair, squinting in the sun with the all-boys soccer team I was a part of. In yet another photo, when I'm probably six years old, I'm in a long-sleeved button-up baby-blue oxford shirt, looking like I'm ready for a business meeting rather than my birthday party at Pizza Hut. Then there's the photo of me as a child, strutting around the house in my underwear, rebelling against the notion that my brothers didn't have to wear shirts but I did. Thankfully, I grew up in a safe home where such subversions of "rules" were appreciated. I was encouraged to question systems, to respond with creativity—and my curiosities were celebrated.

Whether these photos say anything about my identity is only an anecdote compared to the ever-evasive knowing. *Knowing* is elusive and closes down potentials outside of certitudes or declarations. What's more true, more curious, and more exciting is the infinite deep dive into who we are as ever-changing human beings. For those of us who are allergic to definitions: Can we turn inward to unfold our own becoming and blossoming?

This stepping into the spaciousness of our own being will help us hold questions, and also invite questions in. Our curiosity can run wild in the spaciousness of possibility. The infinite expanse of who we are is a place to offer our own unfixed and unmixed attention, a place of prayer, a place where the contemplative life thrives.

BEYOND BINARIES AND SPECTRUMS

I first came to understand the true self, as it relates to contemplative life, from white, male, celibate Catholics who defined the concept in the contemplative Christian context. The phrase *true self* implies there is a "false self." And this is problematic. When such a binary is created, it instantaneously puts up boundaries and limits. But if we queer the true self away from the assumed binaries, we get closer to what the true self means and how it relates to spiritual concepts and identity. Other wordings or ways to imagine the true self-concept include the ground of our being, the truth of our spirit, and the center of our reality as it is enmeshed with the ground of *all* being, or whatever language we use for the Divine. Mystic Howard Thurman writes of "the sound of the genuine in you" and suggests that the sound of the genuine is the "true guide" within oneself.

My understanding of the true self was initially cultivated by the work of the brilliant theologian and author Henri Nouwen, a Dutch Catholic priest; Richard Rohr, a white Franciscan monk and priest whose work has influenced the lives of millions; and

Trappist monk and priest Thomas Merton, a French-born man who took solemn vows as a monk in the middle of Kentucky. Not only did they, as primarily straight-identifying and presumably celibate white men, come from a completely different worldview than I do, they also represented and engaged in systems of oppression, marginalization, and abuse by way of being a part of the Catholic church. (This is not to say that Protestants don't carry systems of oppression, marginalization, and abuse, because they sure as hell do.)

Though I didn't know it at the time, there is so much more to this idea of the ground of a person's being, the truth of a person's spirit, or the center of an individual's reality—beyond the limited and often oppressive views of Catholicism. But slowly and queerly, I recognized that the "true self" concept, much like all areas of contemplation, existed in the margins long before being formalized by these men and their institutions. Like other contemplative concepts and practices, the contributions from the margins are frequently overlooked. This leads to assumptions that concepts like the "true self," accessible by virtue of the presenter's social location, originated with these men. But putting words to a concept or idea doesn't mean you came up with the concept in the first place. And contemplative ideas have been alive for much longer in other groups of people and belief systems, including Hinduism and Buddhism.

My most poignant lessons about the true self have come from those who have experienced marginalization or oppression, those who have existed and persisted in a world that tells them not to. In their lives, their stories, I have learned that the concept of the true self must exist alongside a commitment to liberation. This commitment means that when we listen closely to the ground of our being, we recognize its innate connection to all beings. The true self shows up most authentically when it is dedicated to the well-being of all, amid a deep understanding of oneself. The true self is not selfish; it understands its responsibility to and interdependence with others while also continuously drawing us closer to the infinite well of our own existence, from which we cannot be severed. Black queer Zen Buddhist priest Rev. angel Kyodo williams speaks of this connection of our inward glance and outward existence, saying, "Without practices of self-witness that exist in dynamic balance with the will to liberate the collective, the level of suffering we may bear in exchange is perhaps not even known to ourselves."

The urgency and persistence of deepening our connection to ourselves must also mimic the urgency and persistence we bring to communal care. This has been modeled by a number of liberation movements and was also lived out by the Stonewall Riots of 1969, where Miss Major Griffin-Gracy, a Black trans woman and sex worker, fought back on the front lines against a police raid that led to four nights of rioting. Stonewall is often noted as the beginning of the queer and trans liberation movement. Miss Major Griffin-Gracy's insistence on self, persistence of existence, and commitment to community were expressed in a San Francisco weekly interview from 2015: "I'd like for the girls to get a chance to be who they are. For young transgender people to go to school, learn like everyone else does, and then get out there and live their lives, not afraid or thinking that the only solution for them is death. . . . And when the dust settles, I want my girls to stand up and let people know, we're still fucking here."

Through many stories and experiences, I came to see the different ways folks live into the truth of their spirit by asserting their expressions of gender expansiveness and sexuality, by showing pride in their proclamation of self. And I grew to understand that the center of my own reality was related to my own queerness. Queerness formed a kind of centerpoint for my ever-evolving true self. Queerness is a place of my own unlimited becoming, and its innate connection to the Divine, nature, and my fellow humans.

After all, the true self—the ground of our being, the truth of our spirit, or the center of our reality—must also host queerness. Without the expanse of queerness, how can we expect ourselves to evolve, express, or enjoy the infinite possibilities our spirits require to thrive? How can we expect to pursue the liberation of self and others if we are always tied down by the ideas of society, institutions, or religious environments about who we are?

Everyone carries their own true self in their own way, in their own words, and in their own time. And that is also beautifully queer. My true self is the queer way I rest my ear to the chest of a tree, listening for its heartbeat. My true self is the part of me that shows up at the Indiana statehouse when anti-trans bills are brought to the table, knowing the privilege of my own position as a cis queer white woman and the roles I am called to in communal care. My true self is the part of me that keeps asking questions, stays curious about my own blossoming, and holds myself—and the world—with open hands. The consistencies of who we are also belong to our true selves. Those parts of us that are ever clear, remaining steady and holding fast, are also necessary parts of the ground of our being. They undergird our existence. As we unclench our fists, shedding internalized norms and expectations, we step toward everything alive, toward everything wild, toward the truth of who we are.

CONTINUAL ARRIVALS AND PERPETUAL DISCOVERIES

Writing in the *Journal of Personality and Social Psychology*, researcher Dr. Rebecca Schlegel and her coauthors claim that "expressing the true self is crucial to psychological health." They write that "it seems reasonable to expect that the true self should be related to well-being."

Just as accessing our true self is connected to our psychological well-being, queerness is the gentle welcome into peeling back and examining *who* and *what* that true self hosts. When we queerly glance at ourselves, we release ourselves from the bounds of binaries and even push beyond spectrums. Our true self—that "genuine within" of Howard Thurman—cannot be stagnant and cannot be harnessed. And what will not be idle or controlled calls to each of us for a queerer vision: the true self can be honored, cherished, and continually celebrated as it emerges. It cannot be measured or contained, only treasured.

Examining the true self is also a constant journey into who we are *now*, where we are in this very moment, and the perpetual clarity of ourselves at each passing second. I often get caught up in striving for the future instead of celebrating the moment at hand. One way I am resting in my true self is by continuing to learn and love the gift of the body I am in, in all the ways it appears to me and others. I've begun to learn to love and not just tolerate the space I take up, the presence I hold, and the skin I get to be in.

What exactly does our body have to do with the true self? The body is our vessel, our holy ground, our home on this earth where our true self is housed. Being connected with our body, being embodied, cultivates a congruence with our true self, a congruence that allows our true self to flow more freely, breathe more deeply, connect more honestly, and feel more alive in our chosen, expansive expressions of identity.

Thinking back to my childhood—that bowl-cut I wore for years, the fact that I proudly played sports on otherwise all-boys teams—I tend to my inner child's lack of understanding or acceptance of the true self. As a kid who was always thicker and often taller than most of those around me, sports (before they became too serious) were places for me to express myself outside of expectations and social norms.

But by the time I was ten or so, younger kids sometimes asked if I was a boy or a girl. Their questions annoyed me. But because of society's creation of norms, including around gender, I thought something was wrong with me. It was really the first time I felt pressure to prove my gender in some way, to demonstrate a particular aspect of who I was, and to sacrifice my lack of care on the altar of society's expectations. I wondered if I needed to dress differently, grow out my hair, or play differently at recess.

Alongside this, being bigger than most other kids, I encountered some name-calling. Hearing "fat" on the playground made me even more aware of society's expectations. As a result, I became distant from myself and began to dislike my body, based on society's expectations of what I *should* look like. This kind of "body terrorism" is described by Sonya Renee Taylor as "a hideous tower whose primary support beam is the belief that there is a hierarchy of bodies. We uphold the system by internalizing this hierarchy and using it to situate our own value and worth in the world."

I speak now to that inner child, who at times is still learning to love her body. I remind her that there was never anything wrong with her and that she was bombarded by cultural norms, expectations, and a life script prepared by patriarchy and heteronormativity, a life script created to control her, a life script she would never fit into. To engage with my true self not only meant reconnecting with my own desires and ideas of self; it also meant *dis*connecting from these expectations of harm.

As a cis woman thinking about my childhood encounters, I wonder what trans kids are now experiencing across the country. Not only do these constructs of society not serve any of us; they also perpetuate the misguided beliefs about trans people. One of these false beliefs it that trans people are a threat to cis women and girls. This kind of misinformed and hateful rhetoric leads to the countless laws we now see criminalizing trans people. It's one thing for me as a cis woman to come to understand that the norms placed upon me were indeed wrong, but what does it feel like for a trans person to continually emerge from those norms in a world putting up blocks of hatred at every turn?

As the years passed, I began stripping away my beliefs about myself from these broken expectations and witnessed a significant change. My body, my existence, my identity began to feel more magical, alive, and queer. I continued to release ideas of myself related to society's expectations, and I began caring far more about what feels like *me*—what resonates and reverberates with the ground of my being, what rhythms are in sync with my body. In 2015, while working on the documentary film *In Pursuit of Silence*, I frequently hiked in silence, which helped me love my body's capacity for endurance and appreciate my mystical and often sensual relationship with nature. Going to the nearby

Temescal Canyon, I'd quietly climb to the ocean overlook to feel the elements around and within me. I was refilled with my natural rhythms, recognizing the gift of my body and embracing the erotic energy I carry.

It was on that same trail where I experienced an intimate entanglement with my true self and an interconnectivity to everything alive. As I hiked toward the peak one morning, I unknowingly grabbed my own hand, holding it ever so tenderly. As I realized the affection and love of the moment, I stopped, closed my eyes, and began to weep. While embracing this moment of love between myself, my body, and the beauty surrounding me, I gathered myself and kept walking. I continued holding my own hand, embracing the moment of deep connection between my true self and the world around me. The true self exists in the vessel of our body. And to be in touch with our true self is to be in touch with the erotic, to be in touch with everything alive.

EROTICALLY QUEER

The erotic parts of the self are not limited to the sexual but certainly include it. In the words of psychotherapist and best-selling author Esther Perel, "Eroticism isn't sex; it's sexuality transformed by the human imagination. It's the thoughts, dreams, anticipation, unruly impulses, and even painful memories which make up our vast erotic landscapes. *It's energized by our entire human experience, layered with early childhood experiences of touch, play, or trauma, which later become cornerstones of our erotic life.* We know that even things that give us the most pleasure can come from the most painful sources. Eroticism is not comfortable and neat. It unveils inner struggles, emotional tensions, a mix of excitement and anxiety."

In this way, the erotic includes each area in which we are—or are not—embodied. I am sad about the times I would "warn" my dates about my appearance before meeting them, and I am remorseful for the times I've failed to be vulnerable with my beloved. Embracing the erotic means accepting the stories of once disliking my body, once dismissing my sexuality, and now the ways in which I revel in both. It is the way a particular touch where I once felt wounded awakens me to be fully loved, and to vulnerably accept that love.

The true self, like eroticism, isn't limited to the body, nor to gender or sexuality (or asexuality), of course. But when the true self forgoes the inclusion of sexuality, it falters in its wholeness. And because white male celibate teachers taught many of us in Christian contemplative spirituality the foundation of understanding of the true self, how could we understand sexuality or gender identity/ gender nonconformity as an important part of that? How could I come to understand queerness as a part of my true self until I understood the concept for my own being, my own life?

To engage the erotic as a part of the true self is another way to queer ourselves: to say yes to all we are, all we're blossoming into, and the ways we show up in the world. Saying yes to ourselves is a queer, divine determination to be embodied in each moment.

To bring my embodied and erotic self into the world means learning how to love my body in new ways, to honor its curves and softness, to delight in the ways it is sexual and longs for pleasure, to revere its power and strength, to queerly gaze at its sensitivities and expressions. My body, after all, is a home for my queerness and a vessel for the ground of my being, the truth of my spirit, and the center of my reality. My body is the place from which I seek the liberation of the self and reach out to participate in collective liberation.

The true self continues to invite us all into our own unlimited becoming, which will always be queer, because it is change and growth, inward and outward. After all, the true self has no single advent; it is not the end point on a map of long journeys. Rather, the true self is an individual journey of continual arrivals and perpetual discoveries—a place of unending expressions, where we are free to be alive and awake to be ourselves; where, every day, we are offered new invitations to move closer to the true self's innate presence already within us.

AN INVITATION TO QUEER THE TRUE SELF

Rev. Nicole M. Garcia (she/her/hers)

This interview for the *Queering Contemplation* podcast took place on April 13, 2023, on Zoom.

I came across the work of Rev. Nicole M. Garcia through the work of the National LGBTQ Task Force. She is a queer transgender Latina who is an ordained minister in the Evangelical Lutheran Church in America. When we met up for our conversation on the *Queering Contemplation* podcast, we talked about the ways paying attention to queerness allows for an expansive understanding of the stories and histories that have come before us, as well as the stories within us. Together we also paid attention to the power and importance of reclaiming the term *queer* and why it matters. Here's what Nicole had to say:

I'm sixty-three years old. So that means I grew up in an era where the term *queer* was used as a pejorative. And honestly, it took me a while to warm up to the word, to realize that the word was being reclaimed, particularly by the generation that followed me. I came to the recognition as I was coming out and coming to terms with who I am as a human being, in my sexuality and gender identity, that I would have always been bisexual. I started dating transwomen, and some were post, and some are preoperative, and it was kind of like, *Well, if the individual has a piece or a part like this, or a piece or a part like that, it's just much easier to say, I'm queer.* I'm attracted to an individual that I feel I have an emotional connection to. We share things in common. They are people I want to spend time with. And if we want to have an intimate experience, we can, but it's just too hard to say one thing. So *queer* has become a really nice term for me: an umbrella term.

It also is really a rejection of any binary thinking. Oftentimes the term *genderqueer* is used to say there's a complete rejection of the gender binary. For me, queerness explains my sexual orientation, because I do identify as a transgender Latina. I came from a generation where I was socialized for forty-two years into this concept of very macho male masculinity. And so when I transitioned, I essentially became my mother because of my socialization into that binary. Luckily, I loved my mother. But that's why I use the term *Latina*, because it was an evolutionary process to become the person that I see and know myself to be.

8 | DYNAMIC ENCOUNTER
Queering the Liminal

> A queer spirituality allows for loving pandemonium—
> the challenge of shifts and transitions, the realization
> that we are shaped by each other, and the emergence of
> new identities, new creations within each relationship.
>
> —Mihee Kim-Kort, *Outside the Lines*

Children live in a constant state of novelty. In their repetitive questioning and awestruck wonder, children open up to ideas beyond boxes and thoughts beyond categories. Through their curiosities and imagination, they interpret reality in ways that provide daily reminders of just how queer the world really is.

Being the Titi (my chosen version of Auntie) to four young humans presently spanning the ages of three to ten has been one of the greatest joys of my life. Every day, my niblings (the gender-neutral term for children of one's siblings) show me how the imagination can be a place of prophetic exploration, queer encounter, curiosity, and joy. When the floor becomes lava or a butterfly flutters by, they remind me not only to *look to see* but also to *look to be curious* about the possibilities within each moment and creature.

One of these young humans is Elvis. When I moved to California, I lived next door to Elvis and his family for nearly five years. During that time, Elvis gained a brother named Rocky, and I gained another best friend. Initially, I had no idea how to love, care for, or interact with these brand-new people, but it didn't take long for both of them to teach me in their own ways. Being with them was always the brightest part of my day. From learning how to comfort them as infants to walking outside together to see the sunset, these two taught me more about life, love, and myself than I would have ever imagined possible.

Once, while picking Elvis up from preschool in Santa Monica, I decided to drive us by the Santa Monica statue, created by sculptor Eugene Morahan. Thinking to myself that this would be a great educational moment, I turned left in front of the statue, so he could see it from his backseat window.

"See that statue, Elvis? That's Santa Monica. That's who this city is named after."

As he looked at the large statue standing tall and facing the city with the ocean at her back, he corrected me. "No, Titi, that's God. God's a girl," he said. "Don't you know that?!"

Meeting his imagination with my own childlike joy and wonder—the same joy and wonder he'd shown me so many times—I lifted up my arms in delight at the next stoplight. "Yeah! I don't disagree with you!"

A week or two later, I wanted to check in with this little philosopher, so I decided to drive by the statue once again. Sticking to my old script, I named who the statue was and awaited my correction. This time, however, my backseat teacher calmly replied in a matter-of-fact tone, "No, Titi, that's Buddha."

"Yes!" I replied promptly. Together we allowed the immutable stone of a statue to be transformed by the magic of our imagination. Where, I asked myself, did this freedom of thought, this imaginative creativity, this prophetic philosophy come from? I couldn't recall a single time any of the adults in his world had chatted about Buddha or the Divine as feminine, but I was utterly captivated.

To this day, I'm not sure if Elvis meant the statue was *actually* the Divine feminine or *actually* Buddha or that the statue simply resembled those beings. But for me, Elvis's words were an invitation into dynamic encounter: the place of possibility and liminality. The place where ambiguity lives and binary ways of thinking are challenged; the place where tilting one's head to queer something enlivens and awakens what's before our eyes; the place where a physical statue of Santa Monica can *be* or *become* the Divine feminine or Buddha.

Much like that statue, which seemed so impenetrable, immovable, unchangeable, and solid, I don't often invite the liminality of possibility into those things I find stationary about myself. I've failed to look at my own self with curiosity, especially at things I think have *always* been true about me, those seemingly clear or permanent aspects of who I *think* I am. New, answerless questions arise in me as invitations into the liminality of my own existence:

> How often have I forgone boldness because I'm known to be the "shy one"?
>
> How many times do I bypass my innate masculine expression because of the gendered box of "feminine" I've been placed within—or place myself within?

How often have I opted out of speaking or sharing because
of a perpetuated fear of public speaking?
How much more could I be if I let go of what I was?

Sometimes queering is about permeating the seemingly imper-
meable with questions, curiosities, and wonder. Queering
something gives us permission to see and imagine new ways of
being and to explore with boldness. It is our radical reminder
of just how many things are answerless, infinite, expansive,
unresolved, ambiguous, unfathomable. The act of queering
nudges us to constantly carry life with openness instead of grip-
ping our fists with presumptuous definitions about ourselves or
others.

QUEERLY AND CURIOUSLY LIMINAL

I first heard the term *liminal space* related to specific locations
called "thin places" from Celtic spirituality. The terms are, for
some, interchangeable. Thin places are places where the veil
between this life and the next is so thin that you can sense their
proximity in a new way.

I have a radically unfounded theory that some thin places
exist in the relationship of awe between those close to death and
those nearest to birth. When I see grandparents with their grand-
children, I understand in a visceral way this idea of a thin place.
The grandparent and the grandchild find each other with their
own unique proximity to all that is infinite. There's a conversation beyond words, beyond what is before and after this life, in a
language beyond senses, a language belonging to another plane
of existence.

Liminality, on the other hand, holds even more ambiguity than thin places. It is the between moment: a place where the known opens unto the unknown, a place of understanding beyond binaries, and a place of possibility. According to the *Merriam-Webster Dictionary*, *liminal* comes from the Latin word *limen*, for "threshold"; think also of entrance, doorway, beginning. It can be a place of transition, evolution, morphing, and transformation. Spiritually, the liminal can be a state of gained awareness. Within liminal moments or experiences, I often find myself confused, yet I emerge from these experiences with a greater closeness to and awareness of the Divine. Even—or perhaps especially—when I emerge with fewer answers than before, my openhanded unknowing is somehow a heartbeat closer to the Divine's company, like a shy side-step nearer to her side.

In the midst of the liminal, however, I usually find myself frustrated, like I'm waiting for a dripping faucet to fill a bucket with water. Liminal places can seem daunting and exhausting, but they almost always prove transformative. Those who have described the experience of liminal spaces compare it to the time before giving birth, the borderlands of the nonbinary experience, the state in mystical experiences, and even the spaciousness of the mind.

Driving to see the statue with my nibling Elvis was one instance in which I was invited into the liminal space of the mind and spirit: the place where imagination engages with all that is, all that isn't, and all that *could* be. Elvis walked me to the edge of what was known and offered an example of what could be understood beyond that.

Liminal spaces host the infinite. In a similar way, queerness revels in the enigmatic and in the spaciousness of eliminating binaries. Queerness doesn't exist in the liminal space; it *is* the liminal space. It's the place beyond boundaries and categories where everything is possible and accessible for the imagination and the infinite expanse of our own being.

Because the liminal space engages what we think we know with the imagination, it challenges any certitude. Liminality frees us from our senses to invoke the knowing only found in imagination. Queerness, like the liminal, takes me not only beyond the binary of certitude but through it, and it undermines my exertion of any kind of control—of knowing, believing, defining— over the space, person, moment, or even statue.

In the liminal, no one knows precisely what the hell is going on. And in a way, that is profoundly queer—not because queerness is not *something*, but because queerness is more like *everything* that is loving, just, and liberative. By its very nature, the liminal space—having no set directions, no knowns, and no language— is queer.

But, of course, the liminal doesn't always feel safe. Our imaginations can be terrifying places at times, less full of play than when we were children. Engaging our imaginations, like engaging in silent prayer, might mean we need a trusted companion, a friend, a group, or a therapist in order to safely dive deep into all that might be transfigured in the spaciousness of our minds.

When I consider all the wasted energy I've poured out in my life, all the ways I've made statues of certainty—defining parts of myself, of others, and not making room for the dynamic encounter of all beings—I understand how essential queerness and liminality are for my growth. Together, they reveal our obsessions with definitions and the ways that certitude closes us off from the Divine, and the Divine's ever-expansive image. They remind us of the ways we've used definitions to restrict others' and our own becoming. Queerness and liminality can call forth our imagination, reminding us of the creativity necessary for basic inclusion, for tender acceptance, and for a loving openness to ourselves and each other.

RAINBOWS OF LIMINALITY

It was the morning after the Pulse nightclub shooting in Orlando, Florida, which took the lives of forty-nine LGBTQIA+ people in 2016. I awoke and prepared to walk in the Los Angeles Pride Parade with my church, St. Augustine by the Sea, in Santa Monica—then I heard the awful news. Admittedly, I hesitated about going: Would the Pulse attack amid Pride Month lead to copycat attacks at other LGBTQIA+ clubs and events, including Pride parades? This one, in West Hollywood, was among the most well-known Pride events in the world. But with the courageous path laid out for me by my queer ancestors, I confronted my fears and decided to go. Asserting my own and others' belonging in such a time was perhaps more important than it had ever been.

There was an aura of sadness and fear in the silent air as our church gathered. Taking in the liminality of the moment, we stepped forward into the possibility of pride within it. The morphing of energy was like a desert dust storm coming and going quickly to clear the air. The solidarity and camaraderie, like with most LGBTQIA+ Pride experiences, was tangible.

All the usual opposing suspects were there as well, including representatives of the Westboro Baptist Church, carrying signs like "God hates fags." Police presence surrounded them much of the time, but in the face of such hate, which had perpetrated attacks like the one the night before, the event was all the more emotionally charged.

While we waited to start walking in the parade, groups shared knowing glances: sadness and pride, joy and love, courage and community. I saw Danny DeVito on the *Always Sunny in Philadelphia* float tossing out leis and snapping selfies, the VH1 team excitedly running around handing out their unnecessary freebies, and the Disney team with an ample amount of rainbow Mickey Mouse stickers, which I grabbed for Elvis and Rocky.

When it was our group's turn to begin walking, the reaction to our church's message felt different than in years past. Our simple church signs read "God loves you," "God's love is for all," "God = Love." The messages were not radical, but somehow seemed more moving than they had been in previous years. Upon seeing our signs, people in the crowd mouthed "thank you," were moved to tears, or held their hands to their hearts. Grateful to be wearing sunglasses on this day, I cried, knowing the message held more weight than ever, even for me.

Arriving home after the parade, I made my way up the stairs to see my sweet niblings, who were awaiting my arrival. At the top of the stairs, Elvis greeted me by waving a rainbow flag his mom had gotten, cheering me home.

"Titi!" Elvis exclaimed. "You love rainbows. Why do you love rainbows so much?"

Invited by the small philosopher to answer succinctly, I offered an oversimplified response: "Because rainbows mean 'everyone.'"

LIMINALITY IN THE CLOSET DOORS

My life has been punctuated by liminality—both liminal moments and liminal time periods. The liminal moments have been like those near-mystical encounters with Elvis. They offer flashes of insight where lifeless constructs are thinned out into expansive possibility. The liminal periods of time, however, have been more difficult transformations, spaces where I wonder if I will ever emerge. As with waiting for that bucket of water to fill drop by drop, liminal spaces have often felt like having my permanent home in the unknown. Included in my long-term residencies in the liminal was my experience of not fully expressing my sexuality.

My experience of the closet was one of liminality. It required me to imagine my present and my future differently—to think beyond the boundaries of heteronormativity and patriarchal expectation, and to consider what freedom from the bounds of societal expectation might offer me, aside from a fundamentalist evangelical stance, which was a part of my life at the time.

And while my story doesn't include some grand announcement, the liminality of emergence brought me toward myself and gave me the imagination to cross the threshold out of the closeted life.

For each person in the LGBTQIA+ community, the "closet" experience is different. We have different dynamics of work, family, relationships, and mental and physical safety. Each aspect plays a role in a person's choice to remain or emerge from the closet. And the closet—the place of hiding one's queerness—can be a dangerous place. It is often fraught with fear and has the potential to cause tremendous harm to the psyche. There are times when the closet is necessary for one's safety, physical or otherwise, and there are times when the closet provides a space for waiting until we're ready. The closet is liminal by nature— combining ambiguity and not-yet-ness. Though it doesn't feel comfortable, easy, or sacred, in its not-yet-ness, it is a holy space inviting our truest selves to emerge . . . when we're ready.

THE QUEER BODY'S LIMINALITY

Many years after my own emergence from the closet, while walking along the beach in Venice, California, I listened to an NPR *StoryCorps* podcast episode featuring unexpected advice from a dad to his gay son in the 1950s. His advice moved me to recognize the emotional and cognitive dissonance I'd been feeling: "Don't sneak. Because if you sneak, . . . it means you think you're doing the wrong thing. And if you run around spending your whole life thinking that you're doing the wrong thing, then you'll ruin your immortal soul."

The story and the advice were so moving that I listened to it again and again, recognizing the ways intuitive knowledge of self longs for its safe expression. I understood the hiding and the cost. When I emerged from the closet and stopped the emotional sneaking of hiding my crushes and my sexuality, I began to carry myself differently. It's not that I was donning rainbows or wearing "Queer AF" shirts (though I'm happy to wear that regalia). It's that I was more alive *in* myself because I was finally closer *to* myself and not carrying all the baggage of cognitive dissonance and self-hatred. Out of the closet, I now carry a silent invitation into the wonder of emergence. I began recognizing how my queer body reveals possibility to others and invites others to engage their own curiosity. And now that revelation continues in the way I see my queer body as, itself, liminal.

Once I began to notice the LGBTQIA+ presence all around me, I became more curious about myself and what my life could be. Noticing others who were living as their true, whole selves, in relationship, in marriage, in creating families, in a number of expressions, I felt more possibility than fear. I could finally imagine myself outside the rigid strictures of patriarchy and heteronormativity. As with Elvis's view of the statue of Santa Monica, expansive possibility was ever before me.

Crossing that threshold, I've also learned that the queer body doesn't owe anyone anything. Everyone has their own story, and we each hold it differently. Some people long to make a home in the liminal spaces, celebrating in body and spirit what it looks and feels like to navigate sexuality or gender fluidly, wildly, or ambiguously. Others might feel the vulnerability of passing through the liminal on the way to being recognized as a gender different than the world first assumed. For many trans people in that position, having their discrepancies with social gender norms and expectations pointed out by others can feel isolating, hurtful, or derogatory. The liminal is not home, but a bridge to it. Our relationships to liminality, whether related to identity, sexuality, gender, or something else, can vary in so many ways, often personal and intimate. And while we may be most respectful by keeping our curiosities about others' liminal experiences to ourselves, we are surrounded by people and places that point us back to our own internal journeys. What thresholds are worth crossing? What unknowns call to us?

LIMINALITY'S QUEER RELATIONSHIP WITH MYSTICISM

Liminality is dynamic in its ability to hold so much. It is queer in its reach beyond and through binaries. It is full of imagination in the way it necessitates our considerations of *something else*. For me, one of those many "something elses" was something beyond the closet.

Contemplative life is rich with these liminal moments and time periods. As a place of transformation and growth, liminality meets the contemplative in deep moments of discernment, self-exploration, and compassion. The contemplative's relationship with the liminal is familiar, but never less magical nor easier than the time before.

These days I find myself amid the liminal when my intuition asks me to stay a little longer, look a little more deeply, and consider what *isn't* there as much as what *is*. Sometimes it's enduring a time of unknowing or difficulty in relationship; other times it's continuing a walk in the woods when I'm eager to turn around. Sometimes it's spending hours or days in the hospital with a loved one. In these threshold moments of possibility, I often also find myself encountering the mystical. The unfixed threshold moment becomes mystical in the ways it hosts a grand appointment between ambiguity and the Divine. And that liminality presenting us with a threshold moment always reminds us to open our hands and our hearts, always reminds us to consider what is on the other side.

A monk I'll call Brother Mark once described this kind of liminal, mystical threshold moment to me. He shared about a time when he was unsure about staying or leaving his monastery. He was beginning to wonder if he should leave for a career, a marriage, or an altogether different way of life. And in the liminality of the moment, as he imagined all the possibilities, he went for a walk.

As he walked, he encountered a deer. He looked it in the eyes as the sun was setting, and a sudden clarity formed. "Don't ask me what the connection was. I just had the sense of: 'I've got to stick with this,'" he said. "It was a decisive moment. It was a poetic moment. I couldn't say logically what that image meant or why it meant something. As you imagine, when you come to a threshold like that, there is a great sense of freedom. There was a sense of—if I dig deep in what's here, I am going to find something very valuable, and freedom is one of those valuable things."

I found the simplicity of Brother Mark's story wildly refreshing. He was in tune with my reminder from Elvis: to *look to be curious* about the possibilities within each creature and each moment. In the gaze of a deer, Brother Mark found the possibility of his own being, beyond societal expectations. In the gaze of a deer, Brother Mark discovered his true self as it related to a commitment to place and way of life.

Ultimately, noticing the vastness of possibility within one's life may be the only real information the liminal provides. As queerness invokes the imagination required of the liminal moment, we can sink even more into ourselves, untamed and untethered to definitions. Queerness is the necessary lens to dynamically encounter the liminal space. Queerness is the liminal space.

After Brother Mark told me his story, and as our conversation came to a close, he ever so queerly reminded me of the liminality always before me: "Keep your eye on where you don't know you're going to arrive. Keep your eye on where you don't know you're going to get to. Don't miss the Divine in every day."

AN INVITATION TO QUEER THE LIMINAL

Dr. Elyse Ambrose (they/them/Elyse/El)

This interview for the *Contemplating Now* podcast took place on January 12, 2022, on Zoom.

The work of blackqueer ethicist Dr. Elyse Ambrose has always moved me. Navigating the intersections of race, sexuality, gender, and spirituality, they explore a liminal space based on intersectionality, ethics, and education. I came across their work in our shared experience on the board of enfleshed. In our conversation, Dr. Ambrose reveals the liminality they discovered in their identity:

> In terms of my blackqueerness, the two that I hold together—I make that all one word, *blackqueer* because both of those identities, which are also a politics, a way of relating to the world, speak to me of liminality, of making a way out of no way, of returning to the table to rebuild as frequently as I need to, of recognizing my interconnectedness and the community that makes me, and *I am because we are*—all of that is integrated in the blackqueerness, and it allows me to be open to the mystery of me. And that manifests in my art, it manifests in how, when I collaborate with an artistic subject to bring forth some sort of art piece, it's about when my mystery meets your mystery—what can we create that might speak in a generative way?

9 | UNCOMPROMISABLE PRESENCE

Queering Attention

> Contemplation, for me, is a certain commitment to paying attention to the Divine in all things.
>
> —Cole Arthur Riley, on the
> *Contemplating Now* podcast

True attention, in its rarity and freeness, is queer. Attention is the undistracted self, willing to truly look, deeply understand, and release attachment to moments before or after what is present. Attention is not concerned with naming, capturing, or solving—because attention's primary concern is presence, love, and being. For the contemplative, attention is an inner posture of presence. This posture is not militant or demanding, but is a force of simultaneous effort and surrender.

Paying attention to the Divine within and around us is at the heart of the curiosity that inhabits contemplation. In a world of distraction, it has become a queer kind of thing to pay attention to that sacred presence. When everything around us seems precarious, queer contemplative attention is the disarming nature of witnessing life at the pace of stillness—a pace contradictory to societal expectations. And when that stillness merges with the truth of presence, we are brought to the place of seeing the *is-ness* and *enough-ness* of everything here, because it's exactly where we are, much like the invitation of boredom.

I think about a conversation with my therapist, who prods me with difficult questions (shout-out to all the good therapists out there!). "How would you describe that part of yourself that you want to come out more often?" they ask.

Without hesitation, I say, "Playful, alive, and shy."

"And what would it look like for this 'playful, alive, and shy' self to emerge more?" the therapist digs deeper. Before I reply, they add, "Knowing internally that you have the boundaries necessary when you sense it going too far."

Now I meet my hesitation. *Exactly*, I think to myself, even in the way I pause to control my answer so tightly, keeping all these thoughts inside. Why am I so afraid of that part of myself? The part who longs to be freer and more attentive to the expanse of the present moment. The part of myself who could truly pay attention by pushing away the desire to control, understand, grasp, clench, or even seek comfort in any given situation. The part of myself who is enough in this very moment. The part of me who *is*.

Then, like clockwork, the reel of old stories rolls through my head, delaying my response further. And yet I know that the old stories no longer serve me. When I was only eight, my parents were called in to my school by my second-grade teacher because I was "worrying too much." At that time, few used the word *anxiety* to describe what began for me when I was very young. What's more, my anxiety was compounded because I didn't yet know how to metabolize feelings—my own or those of others that I took on. Instead, I carried the weight of those unspoken emotions with me, often creating a stifled self, unable to pay attention to my internal world, clouded by the emotions of others, too overwhelmed to be in the present moment.

I became the family worrier. Carrying the impossible, I thought I could make everyone around me feel better. I worried so much, as an attempt to help or control, that I hoarded the unspoken feelings and pains around me as if they were my constant responsibility to fix, help, or heal. Every nook and cranny of my life was so consumed by someone else's energy that I left very little room for knowing, understanding, or expressing my own.

Purging, releasing, letting go of this sense of control, developing my own boundaries—cleaning up my internal home—continues to be a long process. I've had to relearn what it really means to pay attention, to get vulnerable and feel feelings, to have a say about what is invited into and what belongs in this house called my body. After all, how can we pay attention and offer presence to the world if we aren't paying attention and offering presence to ourselves?

A part of my own healing process has been paying close attention to those old stories, the ways they've created stifled feelings and shadows to understand and transcend. This inner work of paying attention hasn't been as simple as going through a box of old items, of course. It is much more like a slow and painful ripping off of parts of myself that no longer work, are no longer true, or are causing me or those in my life harm. And these pieces must be paid attention to—they must be seen, held, understood, and released—for me to truly engage with the new story, the gift of the old story, and the healing required for the next healthy step forward. Some of those feelings, through therapy and attention to my inner work, can then come up and out through my voice. Other feelings I return to their rightful owner, or I simply release and discard them, as they are not mine to carry. And many of them—rotten and tethered to false narratives about myself, others, or my life—I simply toss in the trash. They are neither mine to carry nor mine to give or project upon anyone. In those moments, queerly and uncomfortably, vulnerably and softly, I recognize that the gift of attention is a vital part of love.

As I lean into this inner work of paying attention, I come closer to that wild, playful, shy, and alive self—those parts of my healing and wholeness necessary for progress. In these moments, I find myself attending with abandon—sinking my mind, my teeth, and my toes into the present moment without hesitation. There is no longer a need to hold, do, fix, accomplish, create, or produce. I can only offer the fullness of attention to myself and others in its most clarified form. My mind and body are more cleansed of the clutter that never belonged to me anyway. And like most things related to growth and healing, this requires me to practice attention patiently, over and over and over again.

To pay attention, truly and queerly, hasn't just suddenly become my natural mode of operation. It takes conscious effort, vulnerability, and discomfort to release myself from the bonds of old stories, to strip away my old patterns, and to let go into the truth of the present moment. Paying attention requires practice. Zenju Earthlyn Manuel said it this way in an interview on the *Contemplating Now* podcast: "Practicing to be a contemplative, you are . . . learning to be embodied and to be boundless at the same time."

My most alive, playful, and shy self is also my most queer self. Continually being oneself, after all, requires a presence and attention to self, and an acceptance of the lifelong process of evolving, growing, and emerging. Tending honestly to the deepest parts of ourselves and letting go of the harmful stories and expectation of others is one way we can queerly pay attention.

QUEERLY ATTENTIVE

Recently I was on a brief weekend away where I had no cell phone service. I caught myself flailing for something to *do*. The silence was so palpable, I felt my ears tingle with both delight and confusion. I looked for *anything* to fill the void, rather than actually being in the space.

Reaching for the nearest distraction, I found a CD player and looked for some music to play. Ironically, I grabbed a disc titled *Quiet Mind: The Musical Journey of a Tibetan Nomad*, by Nawang Khechog. As I listened, I pretended I was *somewhere* with *something* happening. My hands, addicted to holding my phone, reached for it to fill the emptiness. Remembering I had no cell service, I began to scroll through old photographs, reminiscing about the most recent adventure I had gone on with my partner. She would be joining me later that day, so I began to think ahead to the adventures we might have in this space. Instead of paying attention to the beauty surrounding me and to the precise moment at hand, I looked at my screen, thinking to the past and the future but forgoing the present.

Then it happened: one single bar of cell service. I discovered it in a space near the window. Now I was on a mission to find anything other than myself in a place away where I could finally be found.

Eventually, though, catching up with myself, I remembered *why* I was away. I pushed stop, turned the phone over, and stepped away from the distractions. I went back into the room where no one could reach me—but where I could finally reach myself.

While working on the production team of the documentary *In Pursuit of Silence*, our team interviewed the president of the only multisensory independent design-research laboratory, Steven Orfield. When asked about the role technology plays in our decrease of socialization, he replied, "There tends to be a big technological discussion about computers and whether they're good or bad, and I think that's sort of a silly discussion. But there should be a discussion about how much time you spend in the real world and how much you withdraw."

How much do I withdraw? And what does the term *real world* even mean anymore?

We often find ourselves paying less-than-half attention. We might *think* we're connected to others—through "cares" and "likes" and "loves" represented by buttons on screens—but what if this is another way we are actually withdrawing? Actively and attentively returning to ourselves and others requires a pivot back into the real world. It demands time, focus, genuine presence, and authentic attention. Perhaps queering our attention means first taking our relationships with ourselves and others back off the screen and into the 3D world of presence, company, compassion, and touch.

In a world where attention has become a commodity—as companies literally buy and sell our information as a means to control where we put our time, energy, money, and ultimately attention—genuine attention toward ourselves and others is incredibly queer. Such attention is queer in its rarity, uniqueness, strangeness, and loving presence.

Each day our attention battles with modern life, which insists we make ourselves constantly accessible. If a coworker can't reach us, they text. If we don't reply to a friend's text, they might message us on social media. If our family can't reach us via text or phone call, perhaps they'll open an app to see where we are.

And while most of us crave moments of being unavailable, anonymous, or untraceable, we seem to also desperately fear being forgotten. Is it because in the aloneness and solitude we are even forgetting ourselves? Is it because when we are finally still, we cannot turn our attention inward?

Even now, as I "take a break" from writing, I pick up my phone, like an automatic anxiety-driven bodily act. How could I interrogate my own relationship with the compact glowing box? How might I learn to not reduce my attention to a screen? I begin to ask with the kind of wondering that attentiveness offers: How might I relearn to give this attention of loving presence to myself and others, and to cultivate a healthier relationship with my phone, my computer, my screens?

Seven hours a day: that's how much the average American spends looking at a screen. That figure rose during the pandemic. It's no wonder so many hit burnout. The claims of being "busy" and "productive" have become synonymous with *doing life right.* But the irony is that this screen attention is often barren of the present moment (not always: for some this is the only way they can connect and engage). And our "connections" through screens often leave us feeling emptier and more disconnected than before.

But there's another piece to navigating this new digital world we find ourselves in. During the height of the pandemic, we *had* to figure out a way to queer space so we could be together. Being on screens was how we cultivated community and care. It also revealed the many ways our physical spaces had been inaccessible to people with disabilities, mental health difficulties, or transportation challenges.

The only way to navigate the digital space well is to pay attention to what stirs within us both when we use it and when we put it down. And because we live in a society that loves extremes, we might think taking "social media breaks" will magically create the balance we need. While I think this is a brilliant idea and I've found it helpful for my own life, such a resolution still doesn't solve the need for me to pay attention to my soul and what it is saying to me about where true connection resides—connection with myself and others. Queering our attention in the digital space reminds us of our access to friendships and community beyond the reach of geographic proximity. But it also reminds us to not engage digitally at the cost of physical presence and showing up for one another.

Our anxiety when the screen is turned off gives us important information: that we may be feeling disconnected or alone. Our anxiety when we pick it up offers even more information: clues about what we are striving for, hoping for, needing, or missing. Only when we pay attention, queerly tilting our heads to honestly examine this relationship with technology, can we see what kind of space it takes up in our lives, how it helps us connect *and* how it keeps us from authentic connection. And attention is the crux of connection—we cannot connect or deepen our connections without attention.

Focused attention includes the feeling of being able to see the horizon, the whole picture before us. When my eyes catch up to my surroundings and allow me to see beyond and within the moment, I find flashes of focused attention. In times of deep connection, compassion stirs me to truly know and understand the person before me. On occasions when, untethered to technology, I revel in the beauty of nature, my beloved, a friend, or a family member, I get in touch with my own body, the earth, and relationships. I become attentive to the wisdom of the present.

Often in these moments, a still, small reminder nudges me to remain: *to sink more deeply into this time, to embrace the discomfort of this moment, to deepen my attention here, now.* Then, just when I question the reasons why, the ordinary magic begins to happen: I meet the depth of another or myself with genuine attention, the birds come for a visit, the love with my partner deepens into oceanic oneness, my mind wanders into awe, I experience real rest, and I gather all that is before me without conclusions. This focused attention is contemplative by nature of its merging with and emerging from the Divine.

Reclaiming or redeeming what attention really is becomes another way in which we queer attention. By calling forth genuine attention, we can recover the truth of what is here, now, and enter into an intimacy with the moment, with ourselves, with each other. But this requires an intentional pivot—sometimes away from the screen, away from the multitude, and into singular focus.

THE PACE OF STILLNESS

As I work with my therapist, I am increasingly able to answer questions with authentic attention. "Where do you feel that in your body?" they ask, and I pause to consider the question, truly searching and wondering what is *of* me, my *own* feeling, my *own* experience within my inner world. It's been crucial for me to understand where feelings show up in my body and to engage with them in the loving presence, honesty, and attentiveness they deserve, the ways *I* deserve.

"My stomach," I reply, after scanning other possibilities, none of which seemed to fit. In these moments, there's no doubt a temptation to modify, escape, or enhance. I long to forgo the bodily feeling and try to *think* my way out of it instead of truly understanding and feeling it. Though continuing to learn, I know better now. I was so accustomed to *knowing* feelings that I failed to *feel* them. At times, I didn't yet know how to express them, understand them, or move through them. This old mode of operation has also contributed to the heaping piles of items to discard. I continue to toss out those feelings—and expectations about what to do with feelings— that don't belong in my body. I examine and accept those that belong, welcoming a distilled clarity of self as the dust settles. Paying attention and accepting the truth of what *is*, rather than avoiding or changing it, is no easy task. But these feelings cannot be changed or moved through until they are given attention, metabolized, and understood. Our truth of self cannot emerge until we begin to pay attention to the parts of ourselves that make up who we are.

The more I pay attention, the more I get to encounter the boundless possibilities of stepping into that playful, alive, and shy self who disentangles from the day's worries, comforts, expectations, and distractions. And although those parts of me are indeed shy, they are also the most uninhibited, free, and awake parts—the parts of myself that surrender to the present moment's delights and wonders by paying attention; the parts of myself with an open heart and open hands, relinquishing control in order to be in the moment.

Paying attention is queer not only because of its rarity and strangeness; paying attention is queer because it's the reclamation of our relationship to ourselves, others, and the ways we look at the world. Much like how the word *queer* was reclaimed in the 1980s from its derogatory uses and negative connotations, we need to reclaim paying attention in order for our inner and outer lives—our relationship both to self and to others—to thrive.

Queer contemplative attention whispers an encouragement to sometimes step away from the screen, the noise, the bombardment of the day in order to be truly present to self, others, and the earth.

Queer contemplative attention softly reminds us to listen to our inner worlds and understand what belongs in our bodies, what is ours to move through, what we need to release.

Queer contemplative attention is a reminder to not compromise the moment for something less—for productivity, distraction, modification, or escape. The screen is not the lens through which we pay attention, after all. It is only a tool we use to stay attentive to those we care for and love.

Queer contemplative attention reminds us that this moment *is* and that this moment *is enough.*

Queer contemplative attention is the disarming act of witnessing life at the pace of stillness.

AN INVITATION TO QUEER ATTENTION

Professor Lisa Isherwood (she/her/hers)

This interview for the *Queering Contemplation* podcast took place on August 9, 2022, on Zoom.

I first came across Professor Lisa Isherwood's work while researching body theology and queer theory. As one of the founding editors of the *Feminist Theology* journal, she has helped shape the work of feminist theology over the past thirty years—an impact that will surely continue well into the future. Her writing explores and navigates the intersections of liberation theologies, feminist theologies, eco-theologies, mysticism, queer theory and queer theology.

When I spoke with her, I mentioned her essay "Queering Christ: Outrageous Acts and Theological Rebellions," and read a quotation from it: "The queer Christian body is a transgressive signifier of radical equality. . . . This body lives in the world but is not chained by its narrow definitions and hierarchical power systems." I then asked her if the queer Christian body also lives in a kind of invitational, liminal, or prophetic space. Here is her response:

> Yes, the queer Christian body holds all of those, but with feet planted in the ground. It has to be feet on the ground, because the ground is the reality of where people are suffering. We bring a sort of queer eye on it all, which is about transgression, and is about equality as well, because you're saying, *Yeah, we're all as queer as each other*. We all have a right to our embodied experience.
>
> Look at what's going on in the world—there's got to be another way. And that's what I think a queer Christic eye does. This person of Jesus was in a liberative tradition. So then a queer Christ is someone who's saying, *Yes, and let's expand that, let's see what that could be. Let's transgress in order to see beyond the walls and to see beyond the boundaries to some wider space, bigger space, that is more equal, freer, more life-giving.*

This is what any kind of queer Christology has to do. It has to say, *My body carries something of the Christ nature in it*, with the hope of developing more of that. But in order for that to happen, I have to be free. I have to not feel persecuted and oppressed. I have to have the space to do that. And not just me as an individual, but as people, as groups, we must have it.

10 | EVERLASTING DEPTHS
Queering the Desert

> The Egyptian desert definitely nurtured queer spirituality along with overall Christian monasticism around the third century. The desert was considered barren, but for queer ascetics, it was fertile ground. Separate from the pressures of mainstream society, the desert let them break free from heterosexual norms and conventional gender binaries to follow God's call. Even queer saints from other times and places often found isolated, desertlike places to live as holy hermits.
>
> —Rev. Kittredge Cherry, founder of QSpirit.net

The desert monastics of third- and fourth-century Christianity were some of the original weirdos of the faith. They were monks and ascetics who chose the desert, desiring to be disconnected from the comforts and distractions of everyday life while also embracing the peculiar gifts of desert experience. The desert was a place of less interruption where one could examine the self and step toward the Divine. The desert monastics chose their solitary yet communal lives of prayer, solitude, work, reading, and meditation as daily rhythmic encounters with the Divine and the deepest truths of themselves. Their participation in community was a constant reminder of their innate belonging.

Though the desert may be dry, even for monastics it can also be a place of infinite tears. "Tears," writes Christine Valters Paintner, "are an essential element of the monastic way." Tears reveal the ways we've peeled back the layers of life to the reality of ourselves and the world around us. Tears show us how we've stepped away from ourselves, the Divine, and our inherent connection to all that surrounds us. Tears remind us that the only way to hold anything is with the spaciousness of open hands, with the tenderness of an open heart, and with the delight of the present moment—knowing it can be swept away at any time.

If you've ever been disoriented by an unexpected event, lost someone you've loved, or been heartbroken, you've been in the desert. If you've ever been so grief-ridden that you froze as you looked at the day or moment before you, you've been in the desert. The desert is where we find ourselves hollow, barren. It's where nothing makes sense, where a sudden emptiness haunts us for the journey ahead.

But remembering the desert's innate queerness means recalling the fecundity that can also be found there. Noticing the desert's queerness means glancing up from the arid earth to see the way out—not as a means of escape, but to recall that the barrenness isn't forever, the desolation won't consume us. When we bring a queer lens to the deserts of our lives, we remove our masks and disguises to explore our raw vulnerability as part of the truth of who we are. Only then can we sink our roots of resiliency and compassion through the cracks in the dry ground to commune with others who have felt the same gaping emptiness.

Sometimes we choose the desert. But more often the desert chooses us. In those unchosen moments, we may know how we got to the desert or even participated in our own arrival; other times we just end up there. And though we know that the desert places have plenty to teach us, we often still resist the lessons only found in the empty and barren landscapes of loss.

Joan Didion's *The Year of Magical Thinking* recounts the ways her husband's passing left imprints on every aspect of her life. When a loved one dies, routines must shift, the brain must retrain itself, and the body must let go of the physical presence of the one we most long for even as we carry memories of them everywhere.

In the days of the early Christian monastics, pilgrims living elsewhere who were feeling lost in their daily lives would travel long distances to seek the wisdom found in the desert. I imagine the camaraderie of those pilgrims, walking in the aimless agony of their own experiences of heartache, grief, and loss. From their interior deserts, these pilgrims would travel to the physical desert to beg the monastics for wisdom. "Teacher, give me a word," they'd implore—a word of life! Yet these words of life seem sparse, and often only carry us a singular step through the endless labyrinth of grief.

Deserts are the places of unknowing while longing for answers; spaces of tending to one's wounds while continuing to peel back the scab, just to remember, see, try to understand, or reminisce. Sometimes tending to those wounds means understanding our own participation in them. And during the long, desolate walk, sometimes the words of life are enough for the next steps of the journey; other times the next steps meet an old memory, like a shard of broken glass that tumbled across the floor and missed the broom, sinking into our foot and opening us up once again. Looking for a word of life—a word of survival, an oasis of hope—is natural in these moments. The unchosen desert of grief is an emptiness and boundlessness of wondering if there is ever going to be a way out; it is a place where little makes sense and nothing feels like it will get better. A place where every outstretched fingertip of the griever is absent of our deepest longing, making the descent into darkness a long, slow wander with only the stars to follow.

Sometimes desert conditions invite us to strip ourselves of all that is unnecessary and all that hinders us from forging ahead: the pieces of ourselves that have harmed us or others; the old stories, projections, defenses; the parts of ourselves we've given to others; the woundedness that can make us show up in harmful and hurtful ways. The desert distills us into the absolute rawness of who we are and asks us who we want to be. The desert will always find a way to reveal the core of our humanity, in all its naked vulnerability. And we must live through the desert moments in order to survive. The words of life get us to the next day. The chosen and unchosen deserts must be crossed.

But the desert also invites us to remain and feel, to be still, root, grow, heal, and understand. And as the desert monastics suggest, the only way through the deserts of life is to remain in the practice of examining the self, to stay in the Divine's presence as we unveil ourselves, to truly see and *be seen*. For me, in a very practical sense, these desert moments have led me to increase my therapy, seek the support of friends, and engage in practices and routines to better care for my inner world. It has meant creating new habits, mindful and silent meditation sits, spending less time on social media, and walking miles and miles, in hopes that the Latin phrase *solvitur ambulando*—"it is solved by walking"—is true.

But what do these unchosen deserts *lead us into*? What can we ever expect to get out of such pain?

Some of my desert experiences have brought me close to my most raw, most exposed, and seemingly emptiest self. Yet that is also my most real self. But not all desert experiences are this revealing. Other times the desert gives us nothing as we trudge through the pain. For some, the desert experiences feel more like a dark night of the soul—a kind of crisis of faith. But all these desert experiences have one thing in common: they shoot our roots of humanness down into the ground, where they extend to connect us to everyone else who has ever felt these things. The desert awakens us to the truth of the full human experience, in all its pain, nakedness, and depth.

DESERT ROOTS

The plants of the desert, along with the desert monastics, have plenty to teach us. Desert plants have generated three different adaptive approaches for their parched climates: succulence, drought avoidance, and drought tolerance.

Though substantial, succulents have a fairly shallow root system. But their stubby roots allow them to absorb large amounts of water in short periods, commonly storing it in their leaves, stems, or roots as a means of survival. Drought-avoidant plants give their energy to making seeds, annually living into the cycles of life to escape the harsh conditions. But some of the most resilient desert plants are those that can withstand desiccation and not die. Drought-tolerant plants may need to shed or hibernate in some way, but the depth of their roots, according to botanist Mark A. Dimmitt, "controls opportunities for growth cycles." And while many of these desert plants also take the time to flower, their flowering often happens at night, when no one but the moon is watching.

Even when I don't want the gifts of the desert, I know they are real; with time I will be able to receive them. The unchosen deserts of my life have often been places of my most profound growth, where I've found liminal knowing, healing, new layers of vulnerability, and quiet blossoming. I'm reminded of the words of life that have come to me in past experiences, including the words and wisdom I've received from the early and modern desert monastics.

"The desert way," writes Mary C. Earle, "values going deep, and going deep requires staying put." The desert invites us to stay with ourselves, peeling back the facades of inauthenticity; shedding everything absent of vulnerability, the crux of who we really are, how we really feel. Most of the desert monastics committed themselves to some kind of rhythm combining prayer, self-reflection, and seeking the Divine. And amid this commitment, the landscape of the desert offered its own invitation into depth, growth, and the reminder that we are never alone. The desert plants, like the desert monastics, teach us again of the necessity to deepen our roots. We only carry through the deserts what we must: our reliance on root systems, communal care, and interconnection; the clarity of knowing what pieces of ourselves must die; and the timeless lesson to know and understand ourselves more intimately.

The desert is a place of emptiness, endurance, renewal, blooming, and rebirth—and it demands resiliency. Nature, after all, teaches us that we all have our infinite possibilities and limits;

we all have our places of expansion and contraction; we all have our seasons.

DESERT CURIOSITY

The desert monastics of third- and fourth-century Christianity went away from the world to love it more deeply. They modeled communal care, a commitment to inner transformation, discernment in the spaciousness of silence, and a dedication to simplicity. Like the desert plants, their lives were rooted and resilient, and they had no need to bloom in the daytime for anyone's admiration. Not only did they move away from society physically because they were being persecuted for enacting their beliefs; they also disentangled themselves from the culture of that society. They moved to the deserts of what are now Syria, Israel, Egypt, and Turkey to subvert the oppressive structures of the status quo and to escape an empire of domination. They modeled protest in their movement—by refusing a culture that minimized their beliefs and experiences, stepping into the desert landscape of spaciousness and silence, together.

I've always seen these desert dwellers as an incredible model of protest and resistance. Though in most mainstream writing they've primarily been referred to as the "desert mothers and fathers," their writing, and writing about them, suggests that their lives were free from gender norms and expectations—detached also from society's obsession with binaries. They queered everyday life by stepping aside from expectations, and they queered possibility by revealing a new way to create community, deepen prayer, and develop self-understanding.

In that new community, they supported one another and created a space antithetical to the models of domination. They unfolded their curiosity and unveiled themselves both alone and alongside one another. Those who moved to the desert would either live as hermits or in community with other desert dwellers. But even the hermits often lived in a way that ensured mutual protection and care. Many of the hermit communities were built so that all spaces faced inward. These monastic clusters of cells or caves were named *laura* or *lavra*, after the Greek word meaning "alley," or "narrow lane." There was frequently a church or refectory at the center. This sense of spaciousness and solitude within community is akin to what I've felt in different communities, alongside friends and companions. Together and alone; alone and together. A place of clarity and self-discovery, a place of intimacy and wonder, a place of empathy and compassion, a place of being and rest—a place queerly set apart from expectations.

Amid the daily rhythms and commitments of the desert dwellers, the meaning of the desert was relational—a cultivation of closeness to self, others, and the Divine. But the results were happenstance—nothing was done for the sake of production. Instead, these desert dwellers, consisting of all genders and gender nonconformity, created a kind of economy of their own. Hundreds of books have been written about these desert dwellers' sayings, many of which were brief sentences much like the seemingly paradoxical Zen Kōans of old. And these creative, concise sayings were the words of life sought by countless pilgrims and travelers in need of clarity.

Queering the desert, at least the deserts we choose, is about transgressing norms and forgoing expectations. Queering the desert is receiving a word of life from the emptiness of the moment, the spaciousness of the soul, the wonder of no expectation, and the possibility of our own growth and healing amid our nakedness.

DESERT FECUNDITY

One reason I resist this desert aloneness is that, growing up queer in Middle America, I felt like I lived in a kind of desert. I grew up feeling as if I'd never find my people or my person. So, even when I was surrounded by people, including friends, I felt in my inner world a constant and dull ache of isolation. But where the deserts of our lives arise, there also exist oases of possibility, oases of hope and curiosity, and spaces where we can receive words of life. While growing up, I found such oases in the high school club Spectrum (for LGBTQIA+ students and allies), the gay-owned Italian restaurant downtown, and my high school art room.

In the art room, I found my most fertile times of creativity, my clearest places of discernment, and my most alive experiences of deep connection to self and community. In this space, I painted my curiosity on the blank canvas, reimagined myself in mixed-media pieces, and unveiled my wonder in the chemicals' revelation of the photograph that slowly emerged in the darkroom. In these times I asked myself questions I wasn't even aware I yet had. The stroke of the brush led me to more of myself, and trust in my body's expressions taught me who I was becoming. Writing my story in a stream-of-consciousness manner on the background of my work became a way of preparing myself to paint. Letting go of my thoughts below and layering the colors atop mimicked the way I was letting myself unfold. Coming back into the world from this sacred space became almost like my first meditation practice. I came home to myself and others with an openness to closer connection and a softer stance. In this art room, the other outcasts and weirdos also gathered. We cared for one another and admired each other's inner worlds through our art. We would have lunch together and mull over our days, our thoughts, and our emotions.

Now, my chosen desert places continue to be about entanglement with the Divine, communal camaraderie, and creativity—but they are also places to simply reengage with the truth and nakedness of myself. To strip away the façade preventing me from genuine connection. To find my growing edges exposed, my shadows brought into consciousness, and my inner child healed. Our chosen deserts are often the only places where we slow our pace and disentangle from the pressures of modern life. Amid social media, emails, and constant connection, disconnecting is one way to connect with ourselves and each other. "People who are endlessly available," Walter Brueggemann once shared in an *Encountering Silence* podcast episode, "do not go deep."

SPACE FOR THE WHOLE WORLD

Modern monastic life in the Christian context continues to yield to the importance of aloneness, spaciousness, silence, communal care, and a commitment to simplicity. Contemporary monastics limit their belongings and connectivity to the outside world, and they even choose a landscape set apart from the busyness of life for monastic foundations.

On one of my monastic visits, I stayed at Mount St. Mary's Abbey in Wrentham, Massachusetts, where I met with a nun I'll call Sister Kathy. At the time, she was one of about forty sisters at Mount St. Mary's, a multicultural and multigenerational community. Many of the sisters came from other countries, including Spain, Germany, Korea, Australia, India, Hong Kong, Canada, Brazil, Scotland, and Wales.

Sister Kathy was refreshingly warm. She was from a country across the Pacific where she had originally entered the monastic life and had come to Massachusetts in the 1980s. But her love of the desert in her home country never left her. She spoke of the desert as if it were the irresistible leading character in a romance novel. Sister Kathy felt far from it now, in terms of landscape, but she sensed the same spaciousness of the desert when she went to the community's hermitage. She shared with me that a part of the monastic vocation is the reminder that one cannot just go and take care of everything. The monastic vocation is about staying, remaining, and being still.

Committing to a life of prayer, she explained, didn't mean she was clueless or not participating in the world's difficulties. In fact, most of the monks and nuns I met were regularly involved in learning the latest news of the world. But it was only in this solitude, aloneness, prayer, and even loneliness that Sister Kathy heard an internal voice continually tell her, "There's space there for the whole world. There's space there for the whole world."

In the desert places and moments, Sister Kathy told me, she is never forgotten, and she is never taken from others. Instead, she said, a resonance and connection with others deepens; she feels more entwinement, communal care, and inseparability.

Throughout my travels to these monasteries and in my own learning of balance, I've felt this too. There's a rootedness of connection to others when I center myself in the desert moments of contemplative life, whether they're chosen or unchosen.

There's a softened nature to the vastness of the human experience when I slow myself down to truly see myself, truly recognize
and understand my roles in harm, truly unclench and shed the
pieces of myself unnecessary for the journey ahead.

The deserts are many. Chosen and unchosen desert
encounters have opened me up to see and experience more
room within myself for the whole world—to carry myself, the
beloved, and the world with open hands; with compassionate,
vulnerable, and tender acceptance. From here, I recognize
my capacity for action in the world with deeper clarity about
who I am and what I am to speak—or show up to. My voice is
clarified but softened, and in letting go of my resistance to the
desert, I accept where I find myself, where my heartbeat slows
to the pace of unknowing.

In the chosen and unchosen deserts of our lives, the possibilities of ourselves emerge. In the spaciousness of solitude, we
open ourselves up to the truth of ourselves. We more deeply root,
examine, shed, and soften. Even in the desert moments of daily
life, we are invited into renewal, when the wonder of uncertainty
meets a sacred pause amid a busy day. And almost always, the
desert spaces are places and moments of paradox: knowing
amid the unknowing, refreshment in the parched places, life
amid death, fecundity in the barrenness, midnight blooming, and
acceptance of seasons.

When we recall the innate queerness of our deserts, we
can curiously engage the exposed moment at hand. When
we queer the desert, we can remember that our roots interlace
in community and divine entanglement. When we queer the
desert, we can move toward our own healing, growth, shedding,
and flowering.

As we come to the close of this book, we come not to the end of the inquiry. As Thomas Merton writes in Latin at the end of *The Seven Storey Mountain*: "Sit finis libri, non finis quaerendi," which means "It is the end of the book, not the end of the searching." For queering contemplation is an ongoing search. Queerness and contemplative life remind us of our own companionship for the journey, the many ways our roots deepen to connect and embrace each other, the possibilities of slowing down in our everyday lives, the truth of our innate belonging, and the potential for our perpetual blooming.

When we let go of the contemplative status quo, there are more voices to listen to, more experiences to learn from, and more life experiences to understand. When we queer the things we once thought stagnant, like the monastery or rituals, we can begin to experience the possibilities in practice and encounter. When we queer silence, we can fall into its loving embrace while fighting against its opposing toxicity. When we acknowledge the innate queerness of mysticism and the liminal, we can engage our imagination and eroticism more deeply. When we embrace the queerness of attention and even boredom, we can center ourselves more deeply in the *is-ness* and *enough-ness* of the present moment. When we queer the deserts of our lives, we can rid ourselves of the parts no longer necessary for the journey ahead and stretch our roots of interconnection.

The contemplative life is not a simple path, nor an easy way. It is a commitment to releasing what harms us and others and a determination to increase our compassion and deepen our love. It is a constant slowing down to truly be in the present moment.

As we queer contemplation, and recall its innate queerness, we invite ourselves and each other into infinite possibility. We examine our inner worlds. We commune with the Divine. We dance with each other. And we remind ourselves in the dull aches of life, in our willingness to root deeply, in our moments of focused attention, in our inner sanctuaries: *There's space there for the whole world. There's space there for the whole world.*

AN INVITATION TO QUEER THE DESERT

Rev. Kittredge Cherry (she/her/hers)

This interview for a blog post on cassidyhall.com took place on March 9, 2023, via email.

I first came across Kitt's work when I was a weary queer soul in my twenties, wondering why all the saints and monastics I had heard of and read were largely straight (presenting) men. During a lonely late-night Google search, I came cross Kitt's work on QSpirt.net, where she writes about LGBTQIA+ saints, monks, and nuns, and shares the work of LGBTQIA+ Christian authors, affirming the many ways in which LGBTQIA+ spirituality thrives in monastic expressions. In a conversation I had with Kitt, she shared about her work and her research into the desert monastics. I asked her who some of her favorite desert dwellers of third- and fourth-century Christianity were. Here's what she told me:

> The phrases "desert fathers" and "desert mothers" are too limiting for me, because they reinforce the male/female dualism and use biological parenting as the only model for spiritual mentorship. I prefer to use "desert elders." Often

I simply call them hermits, ascetics, monks, or nuns. Here are a few of my LGBTQ desert elders:

Symeon the Holy Fool of Emesa and John of Edessa joined a monastery together in sixth-century Syria and were united in the "adelphopoiesis" ceremony—the "brother-making" ritual that historian John Boswell calls a "same-sex union." Then they became desert hermits and shared a life together in the wilderness, with all the emotional intensity of a same-sex couple, for twenty-nine years. They parted when Symeon left his longtime companion to live in the city as a "holy fool." We can learn a lot from the way holy fools deliberately challenged social norms for spiritual purposes. Symeon and John also show that same-sex couples can be blessed by God and the church.

Marinos/Marina the Monk has been called a patron saint of transgender parenting. Assigned female at birth, Marina adopted the name Marinos and entered a monastery as a man in fifth-century Lebanon. Marinos embraced a male identity from that point onward, even after being falsely accused of fathering a child. He adopted the boy and raised him as his own son. Like other cross-dressing or transgender saints, Marinos teaches us to see the divine in all people, regardless of gender identity or sexual orientation. I especially value Marinos because this saint is also a loving role model for queer parenting and for integrating parenthood into a contemplative spiritual journey.

ACKNOWLEDGMENTS

Everyone tells you writing a book is hard, but one doesn't find out how difficult until it's too late. Until countless thoughts throughout the day steal your time and fill your notes app. Until pulses of seconds need to be found amid the rush of everyday life. Until plans must shift to create the space and room and minutes to get to that place of momentary clarity. Until the words collide in the mind and heart in just the right way so that a singular sentence can be formed. Writing a book is no doubt a combination of moments that merge to finally bring something to life.

Bringing this book to life was a journey of both this difficulty and my own unfolding. In many ways, this book has been an extended practice in unfolding my inner world and understanding the ways it impacts my outer life. Amid the editing process, many changes occurred in my life that led to more rewriting than I had imagined, but it was necessary rewriting in order to be my clearest and most authentic self.

One thing all writers know is that finding one's unique voice often feels impossible. This book would not have happened without the mentorship and friendship of Jessica Mesman. As a spiritual writer, thinker, and editor, Jessica has always been able to find the seeds of voice waiting to sprout amid the piles of rubbish. In many ways, this book is a result of the piece I wrote and she edited for *The Christian Century* titled "Maybe It's Time for Me to Let Go of Thomas Merton." Likewise, I am indebted to the editing and kindness of Lil Copan, who also took time to help me find my voice and encourage its unique emergence amid stockpiles of other directions I was going in—and hiding myself within. After telling Lil that my experience of queerness was not only about my sexuality but also about the way I tilt my head to look at the world, she reminded me of Emily Dickinson's words, "Tell all the truth but tell it slant." Both ideas became a kind of foundation from which this book, and cover, emerged. My additional gratitude for time and cautious editing goes to Valerie Weaver-Zercher, who guided me to the finish line amid an abundance of distractions and life changes.

Carving away the many moments to form these words took the support of many loved ones, trusted companions, those who picked me up when I was doubtful, and the wise council of those who have inspired me throughout my life. For these and many others, I give thanks: The entire enfleshed board, who were crucial in my final steps—especially co-directors Robert Monson, M Jade Kaiser, and Anna Blaedel. Amanda Thrasher and her cat Papi (who basically coauthored the book with all his lap-cuddling hours). Kerry Connelly, Anne Garner, Shaleen Kendrick, Laura Jean Truman, Patrick Shen, Yael R. Shinar, the Rev. Dr. Sarah Griffith Lund, the Rev. Dr. Scott Seay, Mary Bishop, Shana Hutchings, Judith Lyons, and Deb Giordano. All of my Patreon supporters over the years, and the countless others who have shown up for me along the way.

I am also indebted to all the queer contemplative ancestors and present-day wisdom found in this book, including the interviewees throughout the book: Alicia Crosby Mack, Jes Kast,

ACKNOWLEDGMENTS

Kevin Quashie, Miguel H. Díaz, Mihee Kim-Kort, Assata de la Cruz, Nicole Garcia, Elyse Ambrose, Lisa Isherwood, Kittridge Cherry, and the many others before and after me.

Every day, I wake up and see a small reminder from e. e. cummings that I've taped to my wall: "It takes courage to grow up and become who you are." This courage comes from the smallest ones in my life. Since first having niblings, I have become captivated by the beauty of growing up to become who we are. Seeing the intricacies of their lives, the little and incredible things that make them unique, has also helped my own unfolding, my own queerness, my own understanding of self, and my own growth. For these precious souls, who teach me time and time again, I give thanks: Elvis, Rocky, Huckleberry, and Happy (yes, those are all their real names). Alongside them, I have had the support of a family who encourages my weird adventures and cheers me on with love. For them, I give thanks: Mom Hall, Dad Hall, Richard Hall, Hiland Hall, Leslie Hall, Lauren Thompson Hall, and Kate Hall.

NOTES

CHAPTER 1

1 ***My therapist tells me I'm a plant:*** Portions of this chapter are adapted from Cassidy Hall, "Maybe It's Time for Me to Let Go of Thomas Merton," *Christian Century*, December 1, 2021; and Cassidy Hall, "Awakening Mysticism with the Scholarship of African American Women" (master's thesis, Christian Theological Seminary, 2021).

4 ***"Contemplation is not confined":*** Barbara A. Holmes, *Joy Unspeakable: Contemplative Practices of the Black Church*, 2nd ed. (Minneapolis: Fortress, 2017), 183–184; 113.

4 ***the ways the contemplative path comes to fulfillment:*** James Finley, *Thomas Merton's Path to the Palace of Nowhere* (Boulder, CO: Sounds True, 2004), audiobook.

4 ***"devotion to revealing":*** B. Alan Wallace, *Mind in the Balance: Meditation in Science, Buddhism, and Christianity*, The Columbia Series in Science and Religion (New York: Columbia University Press, 2009), Kindle loc. 234.

5 ***Dr. Holmes speaks of:*** Paul Swanson, "Dr. Barbara Holmes from 2016 in Celebration of the Revised Edition of Her Book, *Joy Unspeakable*," *Contemplify* (podcast), October 17, 2017, https://contemplify.com/2017/10/17/bonus-episode-barbara-holmes-from-2016-in-celebration-of-the-revised-edition-of-her-book-joy-unspeakable/.

NOTES

5 ***The assumption that contemplative practice requires silence:*** Bernard McGinn, *The Presence of God: A History of Western Christian Mysticism* (New York: Crossroad, 1991), 45.

5 ***"we have drawn the spiritual veil":*** Holmes, *Joy Unspeakable*, 20.

9 ***"In other words, the pitch":*** Thomas Merton and Robert E Daggy, *The Road to Joy: The Letters of Thomas Merton to New and Old Friends*, 1st Harvest/HBJ ed. (San Diego: Harcourt Brace Jovanovich, 1993), 345.

11 ***"contemplative practices of the Black Lives Matter movement":*** Holmes, *Joy Unspeakable*, x.

12 ***an understanding of Harriet Tubman as a contemplative mystic:*** Therese Taylor-Stinson, *Walking the Way of Harriet Tubman: Public Mystic and Freedom Fighter* (Minneapolis: Broadleaf, 2023).

14 ***"They can have Thomas Merton":*** Thomas Merton, *The Sign of Jonas* (San Diego: Harcourt, 1981), 253.

15 ***flowers have often symbolized or referenced queer folks:*** Sarah Prager, "Four Flowering Plants That Have Been Decidedly Queered: The Queer History of the Pansy and Other Flowers," *JSTOR Daily*, January 29, 2020; Christobel Hastings, "How Lavender Became a Symbol of LGBTQ Resistance," *CNN Style*, June 4, 2020.

CHAPTER 2

23 ***"It was the feeling all the time":*** Andrew Solomon, "Depression, the Secret We Share," *TEDxMet*, October 2013, www.ted.com/talks/andrew_solomon_depression_the_secret_we_share.

24 ***"Many poets are not poets":*** Thomas Merton, "Integrity," *New Seeds of Contemplation* (1961; repr., New York: New Directions, 2007), 98. Emphasis added.

25 ***Given the abuse that has occurred in some monastic spaces:*** "The Overlooked Scandal of Priests Sexually Abusing

Nuns," interview with Laurie Goodstein, on *The Daily* (podcast), February 7, 2019, produced by Michael Simon Johnson and Ike Sriskandarajah, https://www.nytimes.com/2019/02/07/podcasts/the-daily/pope-nuns-priests-sexual-abuse.html?showTranscript=1.

26 ***"the ending is indeed an ending":*** "Night Prayer (Compline)," The Church of England, accessed September 3, 2023, https://www.churchofengland.org/prayer-and-worship/worship-texts-and-resources/common-worship/daily-prayer/night-prayer-compline.

29 ***"monk" comes from the Greek*** **monos***:* Merriam-Webster.com *Dictionary*, s.v. "monk," https://www.merriam-webster.com/dictionary/monk; s.v. "nun," https://www.merriam-webster.com/dictionary/nun. See also *Wiktionary*, s.v. "nonnus," https://en.wiktionary.org/wiki/nonnus#:~:text=Noun,old%20man. All accessed October 9, 2023.

30 ***"Not Queer like gay":*** Sonya Renee Taylor, *The Body Is Not an Apology: The Power of Radical Self-Love*, 2nd ed. (Oakland, CA: Berrett-Koehler, 2021), 116–117.

32 ***"What happens with me is":*** Cassidy Hall, "Patient Endurance: A Conversation with Sister Barbara Jean LaRochester," *Contemplating Now* (podcast), March 27, 2021, https://cassidyhall.com/2021/03/27/patient-endurance-a-conversation-with-sister-barbara-jean-larochester/.

35 ***"I determine to live the outer life":*** Howard Thurman, *Meditations of the Heart* (Boston: Beacon, 2014), 174–175.

CHAPTER 3

41 ***This organization, which sought to change people with "same-sex attraction":*** HRC Foundation, "The Lies and Dangers of Efforts to Change Sexual Orientation or Gender Identity," Human Rights Campaign, accessed August 30, 2023, https://tinyurl.com/4vye8txp; Victoria Whitley-Berry, Sarah

McCammon, "Former 'Ex-Gay' Leaders Denounce 'Conversion Therapy' in a New Documentary," *Morning Edition*, NPR, August 2, 2021, www.npr.org/2021/08/02/1022837295/former-ex-gay-leaders-denounce-conversion-therapy-in-a-new-documentary August 2.

41 ***Thankfully, toxic silences can be transformed:*** David France, "Pictures from a Battlefield," *New York Magazine*, March 23, 2012, https://nymag.com/news/features/act-up-2012-4/.

43 ***"not only my self-identity; it is also":*** Pamela R. Lightsey, *Our Lives Matter: A Womanist Queer Theology.* (Eugene: Wipf & Stock, 2015), ix.

45 ***the sixth-century monks of Iona:*** Kenneth Steven, "Iona Was Once the Beating Heart of Celtic Christianity," *Christian Century*, March 9, 2022, https://www.christiancentury.org/article/first-person/iona-was-once-beating-heart-celtic-christianity.

49 ***"Silence is God's first language":*** Thomas Keating, *Invitation to Love: The Way of Christian Contemplation*, 20th Anniversary Edition (London: Bloomsbury, 2012), 105.

49 ***The prayer practice takes place in four steps:*** "Centering Prayer," *Contemplative Outreach*, accessed August 31, 2023, www.contemplativeoutreach.org/centering-prayer-method.

52 ***"Silence often denotes something":*** Kevin Everod Quashie, *The Sovereignty of Quiet: Beyond Resistance in Black Culture* (Piscataway: Rutgers University Press, 2012), 22, 113, 116.

CHAPTER 4

53 ***"I think people have mystical experiences all the time":*** Cassidy Hall, "Fresh Courage: A Conversation with Dr. Lerita Coleman Brown," *Contemplating Now* (podcast), May 30, 2021.

54 ***"All mysticism is a part of the endeavor to escape":*** Dorothee Sölle, *The Silent Cry: Mysticism and Resistance* (Minneapolis: Fortress, 2001), Kindle loc. 892–93.

54 *"along with gender":* Joy R. Bostic, *African American Female Mysticism: Nineteenth-Century Religious Activism* (New York: Palgrave Macmillan, 2013), 29.

55 *"Mutual dependence is the fundamental model":* Sölle, *The Silent Cry*, Kindle loc. 4027.

55 *"a leader whose interiority":* Barbara A. Holmes, *Joy Unspeakable: Contemplative Practices of the Black Church*, 2nd ed. (Minneapolis: Fortress, 2017), 125.

55 *mysticism is authentic only when:* Bostic, *African American Female Mysticism*, 40.

56 *"opens the door for understanding not only the erotic elements":* Miguel H. Díaz, *Queer God de Amor (Disruptive Cartographers: Doing Theology Latinamente)* (New York: Fordham University Press, 2022), 9.

56 *"would take out my bruises":* Howard Thurman, *With Head and Heart: The Autobiography of Howard Thurman* (San Diego: Harcourt Brace, 1979), 9.

56 *"I had a tree outside my window":* Cassidy Hall, "Speaking Down Barriers: A Conversation with Poet Davelyn Hill," *Contemplating Now* (podcast), October 27, 2021.

59 *"The poet cannot make the poem happen":* James Finley, "Thomas Merton: Mystic Teacher for Our Age," *The Merton Annual* 28 (2015), 181–195.

60 *"Contemplation is the mystic's medium":* Evelyn Underhill, *Mysticism: A Study of the Nature and Development of Man's Spiritual Consciousness* (1977; repr., n.p.: e-artnow, 2018), Kindle loc. 5624.

60 *Eros, the Greek god of love:* "Eros/Amor/Cupid," Rijksmuseum, Amsterdam (website), www.rijksmuseum.nl/en/rijksstudio/subjects/erosamor/cupid.

61 *"the vital energy that courses through the world":* Evelyn Eaton Whitehead and James D. Whitehead, *Holy Eros: Pathways to a Passionate God* (Maryknoll, NY: Orbis Books, 2009), Kindle loc. 9–10.

62 **"seeking the ineffable in the ordinary":** Holmes, *Joy Unspeakable*, 124.

63 **"who invite Spirit's guidance":** Lerita Coleman Brown, *What Makes You Come Alive: A Spiritual Walk with Howard Thurman* (Minneapolis: Broadleaf, 2023), 153. Emphasis in the original.

63 **"compelled to respond to this encounter":** Bostic, *African American Female Mysticism*, 25.

63 **"Resistance is not the outcome of mysticism":** Sölle, *The Silent Cry*, Kindle loc. 2686.

64 **"borrowed the eyes of God":** Sölle, *The Silent Cry*, Kindle loc. 3983.

64 **When we queer mysticism:** Portions of this chapter are from Cassidy Hall, "Awakening Mysticism with the Scholarship of African American Women" (master's thesis, Christian Theological Seminary, 2021).

CHAPTER 5

68 **"constantly disrupts the established norm":** Miguel A. De La Torre, *Burying White Privilege: Resurrecting a Badass Christianity* (Grand Rapids: Eerdmans, 2019), 142.

68 **"A closed system is a trap":** Maggie Ross, "The Tears of Conversion," *Monastic Studies* 18 (Christmas 1998): 211.

69 **Ethnographer Arnold van Gennep:** Arnold van Gennep, *The Rites of Passage* (Chicago: University of Chicago Press, 1960).

70 **The innate belonging of LGBTQIA+ folks:** For more on this topic, see Linn Marie Tonstad, *Queer Theology: Beyond Apologetics* (Eugene, OR: Cascade, 2018).

72 **"crucial aspect of converting":** Gabriele vom Bruck and Barbara Bodenhorn, eds., *The Anthropology of Names and Naming* (Cambridge: Cambridge University Press, 2006), Kindle loc. 97–101.

72 **In psychological discourse, naming is considered:** Pauline J. Horne and C. Fergus Lowe, "On the Origins of Naming and Other Symbolic Behavior," *Journal of the Experimental Analysis of Behavior* 65, no. 1 (January 1996): 185–241.

73 ***"proper names are never simply there"***: Bodenhorn and vom Bruck, *The Anthropology of Names and Naming*, Kindle loc. 1816.

73 ***"each participant has a well-rehearsed role"***: Felicitas D. Goodman, *Ecstasy, Ritual, and Alternate Reality: Religion in a Pluralistic World* (Bloomington: Indiana University Press, 1988), 31.

73 ***"to serve as a pronoun"***: Ezra Marcus, "A Guide to Neopronouns," *New York Times*, April 8, 2021, www.nytimes.com/2021/04/08/style/neopronouns-nonbinary-explainer.html.

77 ***"If you want to"***: Reza Aslan, "Why I Am a Muslim," *CNN*, April 19, 2017, https://www.cnn.com/2017/02/26/opinions/believer-personal-faith-essay-reza-aslan/index.html#:~:text=Different%20words%2C%20same%20thing, with%20in%20expressing%20my%20faith.

78 ***"Queerness begins from the premise"***: Mihee Kim-Kort, *Outside the Lines: How Embracing Queerness Will Transform Your Faith* (Minneapolis: Fortress, 2018), 74.

CHAPTER 6

82 ***"And if that becomes boring, good"***: Full interview transcript with Dr. Helen E. Lees can be found in: Patrick Shen and Cassidy Hall, *Notes on Silence* (Arcadia, CA: Transcendental Media, 2018), 149.

83 ***keep a small skull on our desk***: Ruth Graham, "Meet the Nun Who Wants You to Remember You Will Die," *New York Times*, May 14, 2021, https://www.nytimes.com/2021/05/14/us/memento-mori-nun.html.

84 ***Assumption Abbey was undergoing a new and dramatic change***: See the Assumption Abbey website: www.assumptionabbey.org/transition.

84 ***The monks at Holy Trinity Abbey in Huntsville, Utah***: Brian Maffly, "Huntsville Monastery Has Faded Away, but Preservation Prayers Have Been Answered for Its Farm Fields," *Salt Lake Tribune*,

April 15, 2021, www.sltrib.com/news/environment/2021/04/15/ huntsville-monastery-has/.

86 *Acedia is a kind of spiritual apathy:* Merriam-Webster. com Dictionary, s.v. "acedia," accessed September 3, 2023, www. merriam-webster.com/dictionary/acedia.

86 *Used in monastic and medieval literature:* Kathleen Norris, *Acedia & Me: A Marriage, Monks, and a Writer's Life* (New York: Penguin, 2008), 2, 26.

87 *"restless boredom, frantic escapism":* Norris, *Acedia & Me*, 4, 130.

88 *we may need to reach out to a therapist:* The 988 Lifeline is now active across the United States (call or text). National Alliance on Mental Illness (nami.org) information and referral services: 1-800-950-NAMI (6264). The Trevor Project hotline offers support for LGBTQIA+ youth and families struggling with mental health challenges at 1-866-4-U-TREVOR (488-7386) and www. theTrevorProject.org.

89 *what many studies reveal about boredom:* Karen Gasper and Brianna L. Middlewood, "Approaching Novel Thoughts: Understanding Why Elation and Boredom Promote Associative Thought More Than Distress and Relaxation," *Journal of Experimental Social Psychology* 52 (May 2014): 50–57.

90 *"One night, Jim asked if he might do the dishes":* Thich Nhat Hanh, *The Miracle of Mindfulness: An Introduction to the Practice of Meditation* (Boston: Beacon, 1996), 7. See also the retelling from Jim's perspective: "A Few Memories of Thich Nhat Hanh," *Jim and Nancy Forest* (website), January 11, 2012, https://jimandnancyforest. com/2012/01/nhat-hanh/.

CHAPTER 7

98 *"I know in my heart":* Thomas Merton, in *Day of a Stranger* (documentary), dir. by Cassidy Hall (2021). Used with permission from Now You Know Media, Merton Center recording #214-10.

98 *As an enneagram 5:* For more information about enneagrams, see Don Richard Riso and Russ Hudson, *The Wisdom of the Enneagram: The Complete Guide to Psychological and Spiritual Growth for the Nine Personality Types* (New York: Bantam, 1999).

99 *Maybe when sexuality and gender forgo binary expectations:* Learn more about the history of nonbinary science from and follow @alokvmenon on Instagram. See also Joanne J. Meyerowitz, *How Sex Changed: A History of Transsexuality in the United States* (Cambridge, MA: Harvard University Press, 2004).

100 *"the sound of the genuine in you":* Howard Thurman, "The Sound of the Genuine (Baccalaureate Ceremony) (Spelman College), 1980 May 4," *The Howard Thurman Digital Archive*, accessed September 4, 2023, https://thurman.pitts.emory.edu/items/show/838.

102 *"Without practices of self-witness":* angel Kyodo williams, Lama Rod Owens, and Jasmine Syedullah, *Radical Dharma: Talking Race, Love, and Liberation* (Berkeley, CA: North Atlantic, 2016), xvi.

102 *"I'd like for the girls to get a chance":* Julia Carrie Wong, "Miss Major: The Bay Area's Trans Formative Matriarch," *SF Weekly*, July 22, 2015, http://web.archive.org/web/20170312032451/http://archives.sfweekly.com/sanfrancisco/news-san-francisco-transgender-lgbt-stonewall-sex-work-prison/Content?oid=38 46678&showFullText=true. See also Mason Funk, Interview with Miss Major Griffin-Gracy, *Outwords*, July 27, 2016, https://theoutwordsarchive.org/interview/miss-major-griffin-gracy/ and Toshio Meronek and Miss Major Griffin-Gracy, *Miss Major Speaks: Conversations with a Black Trans Revolutionary* (London: Verso, 2023).

104 *"expressing the true self is crucial":* Rebecca J. Schlegel, Joshua A Hicks, Jamie Arndt, and Laura A. King, "Thine Own Self: True Self-Concept Accessibility and Meaning in Life," *Journal of Personality and Social Psychology* 96, no. 2 (2009)): 473–490, https://doi.org/10.1037/a0014060.

105 *"a hideous tower whose primary support beam":* Sonya Renee Taylor, *The Body Is Not an Apology: The Power of Radical*

Self-Love, 2nd ed. (Oakland, CA: Berrett-Koehler Publishers, 2021), Kindle loc. 1158.

108 ***"Eroticism isn't sex":*** Esther Perel, "Why Eroticism Should Be Part of Your Self-Care Plan," *Esther Perel* (blog), accessed September 4, 2023, https://www.estherperel.com/blog/eroticism-self-care-plan. Emphasis added.

CHAPTER 8

111 ***my niblings (the gender-neutral term for children of one's siblings):*** The gender-neutral terms *niblings* for children of one's siblings and *piblings* for siblings of one's parent were created in the 1950s by Samuel E. Martin, a professor of Korean linguistics. "Words We're Watching: Nibling," Merriam-Webster.com *Dictionary*, accessed September 4, 2023, www.merriam-webster.com/words-at-play/words-were-watching-nibling. However, the number of alternatives and ways of describing family relations have become vast: Wren Sanders, "How to Refer to Your Nonbinary Family Members," *them*, November 24, 2021, www.them.us/story/nonbinary-familial-terms-nibling-pibling-auncle-guide.

115 ***According to the* Merriam-Webster Dictionary:** *Merriam-Webster.com Dictionary*, s.v. "liminal," accessed September 5, 2023, https://www.merriam-webster.com/dictionary/liminal.

115 ***Those who have described:*** Courtney E. Martin, "The Liminal Space before Giving Birth," *On Being*, July 22, 2016. onbeing.org/blog/the-liminal-space-before-giving-birth/.

115 ***the borderlands of the nonbinary experience:*** Nyk Robertson, "The Power and Subjection of Liminality and Borderlands of Non-Binary Folx," *Gender Forum*, accessed September 5, 2023, https://tinyurl.com/2dt3zm9v.

119 ***Each aspect plays a role:*** Alexandra Suppes, Jojanneke van der Toorn, Christopher T. Begeny, "Unhealthy Closets, Discriminatory Dwellings: The Mental Health Benefits and Costs of Being Open about One's Sexual Minority Status," *Social Science & Medicine* 285 (2021): 114286, https://tinyurl.com/y9sc82js.

120 ***"Don't sneak":*** NPR Staff, "'Don't Sneak': Dad's Unexpected Advice to His Gay Son in the '50s," NPR *StoryCorps,* June 27, 2014, https://tinyurl.com/37b4k5hz.

CHAPTER 9

128 ***"Practicing to be a contemplative":*** Cassidy Hall, "Embodied and Boundless: A Conversation with Zenju Earthlyn Manuel," *Contemplating Now* (podcast), April 24, 2021, https://cassidyhall.com/2021/04/24/embodied-and-boundless-a-conversation-with-zenju-earthlyn-manuel/.

130 ***"There tends to be a big technological discussion":*** Patrick Shen, dir., Interview with Steven Orfield for *In Pursuit of Silence* (documentary), Transcendental Media, 2015.

131 ***Seven hours a day:*** Rebecca Moody, "Screen Time Statistics: Average Screen Time in US vs. the Rest of the World," *Comparitech,* March 15, 2023, https://www.comparitech.com/tv-streaming/screen-time-statistics/.

136 ***"The queer Christian body":*** Lisa Isherwood, "Queering Christ: Outrageous Acts and Theological Rebellions," *Literature and Theology* 15, no. 3 (2001): 249–261.

CHAPTER 10

140 ***"Tears," writes Christine Valters Paintner:*** Christine Valters Paintner, *Desert Fathers and Mothers: Early Christian Wisdom Sayings—Annotated and Explained* (Woodstock, VT: SkyLightPaths, 2012), Kindle loc. 1518.

141 ***"Teacher, give me a word":*** Valters Paintner, *Desert Fathers and Mothers* Kindle loc. 498.

142 ***the Latin phrase solvitur ambulando:*** *Merriam-Webster.com Dictionary,* s.v. "solvitur ambulando," accessed June 13, 2023, www.merriam-webster.com/dictionary/solvitur%20ambulando.

144 ***the depth of their roots, according to botanist Mark A. Dimmitt:*** Mark A. Dimmitt, "How Plants Cope with the Desert

Climate," *Sonorensis* 17, no. 1 (Spring 1997): http://www.hummingbirds.arizona.edu/Courses/ecol414_514/readings/cope_dimmitt.pdf.

144 ***"The desert way," writes Mary C. Earle:*** Mary C. Earle, *The Desert Mothers: Spiritual Practices from the Women of the Wilderness* (Harrisburg, PA: Morehouse, 2007), 31.

145 ***The desert monastics:*** Laura Swan, *The Forgotten Desert Mothers: Sayings, Lives, and Stories of Early Christian Women* (Mahwah, NJ: Paulist, 2001).

146 **laura *or* lavra:** *The Oxford Dictionary of Byzantium,* s.v. "lavra" (New York: Oxford University Press, 1991).

148 ***"People who are endlessly available":*** Walter Bruggeman, "An Orientation to Silence," *Encountering Silence* (podcast), November 27, 2019, https://podcasts.bcast.fm/e/pnmr34m8.

151 ***"Sit finis libri, non finis quaerendi":*** Thomas Merton, Robert Giroux, and William H Shannon, *The Seven Storey Mountain*, 50th anniv. ed. (New York: Harcourt Brace, 1998), 462.

ACKNOWLEDGMENTS

156 ***"Tell all the truth but tell it slant":*** Emily Dickinson, *The Poems of Emily Dickinson*, ed. R. W. Franklin (Cambridge: Harvard University Press, 2005), 737.

157 ***"It takes courage to grow up":*** Matthew Burgess and Kris DiGiacomo, *Enormous Smallness: A Story of E. E. Cummings*, 1st ed. (New York: Enchanted Lion Books, 2015).